THE
BEATITUDES

by

HUGH MARTIN

HARPER & BROTHERS

Publishers, New York

Library of Congress Catalog Card Number: 52-11077

THE
BEATITUDES

CONTENTS

THE BEATITUDES OF JESUS

As recorded in

Matthew 5.1-12

And seeing the multitudes, he went up into a mountain: and when he was set, his disciples came unto him:

And he opened his mouth, and taught them, saying,

Blessed are the poor in spirit: for theirs is the kingdom of heaven.

Blessed are they that mourn: for they shall be comforted.

Blessed are the meek: for they shall inherit the earth.

Blessed are they which do hunger and thirst after righteousness: for they shall be filled.

Blessed are the merciful: for they shall obtain mercy.

Blessed are the pure in heart: for they shall see God.

Blessed are the peacemakers: for they shall be called the children of God.

Blessed are they which are persecuted for righteousness' sake: for theirs is the kingdom of heaven.

Blessed are ye, when men shall revile you, and persecute you, and shall say all manner of evil against you falsely, for my sake.

Rejoice, and be exceeding glad: for great is your reward in heaven: for so persecuted they the prophets which were before you.

Luke 6.20-26

And he lifted up his eyes on his disciples, and said, Blessed be ye poor: for yours is the kingdom of God.

Blessed are ye that hunger now: for ye shall be filled. Blessed are ye that weep now: for ye shall laugh.

Blessed are ye, when men shall hate you, and when they shall separate you from their company, and shall reproach you, and cast out your name as evil, for the Son of man's sake.

Rejoice ye in that day, and leap for joy: for, behold, your reward is great in heaven: for in the like manner did their fathers unto the prophets.

But woe unto you that are rich! for ye have received your consolation.

Woe unto you that are full! for ye shall hunger. Woe unto you that laugh now! for ye shall mourn and weep.

Woe unto you, when all men shall speak well of you! for so did their fathers to the false prophets.

I

THE BEATITUDES IN GENERAL

> Who is the happy warrior? Who is he
> That every man in arms would wish to be?

AND the poet goes on to give a not unworthy answer, that stirs the soul every time it is re-read.[1] Poets, philosophers and religious teachers in all the generations have asked that question in varying phrase and have offered their answers. Who is the happy man? Who understands the secret of true living? What kind of life is most worth living? We may think of the Beatitudes as the answer Jesus gave.

1

One of the great difficulties here, as so often in trying to understand the New Testament, is with the devaluation, or even the change of meaning of words. A great effort is needed in reading St. Paul's great hymn of love in the Authorised Version to break away from the debased associations of the word 'charity'. So this word 'blessed' has become rather a sanctimonious, musty, remote word. Yet what is to be put in its place? 'Happy' suggests a state too superficial and light-hearted to convey the idea. 'There is in man', wrote Thomas Carlyle, in *Sartor Resartus*, 'a Higher than Love of Happiness: he can do without Happiness and instead thereof find Blessedness.' Happiness, we might say, depends on the things that *happen* to us. Blessedness is deeper, it is a matter of character, it can transmute what happens. The Greek word used here, *makarios*, is not

[1] William Wordsworth, *The Character of the Happy Warrior*. Compare the poems by Campion and Wotton, 'The man of life upright,' and 'How happy is he born and taught.'

the usual word for happiness, but is the one employed in classical Greek by both poets and philosophers for the attainment of life's ideal, the *summum bonum*. 'Blessedness', says a note in *Weymouth's New Testament*, 'is of course an infinitely higher and better thing than mere happiness. People who are blessed may outwardly be much to be pitied, but from the higher and truer standpoint they are to be admired, envied, congratulated and imitated.' There is a helpful suggestion here. Jesus is offering congratulations. The man who lives like this, He says, is getting the best out of life, living the kind of life that is really worth while. Branscomb[1] says the word is in fact used in contemporary private letters in expressions of warmest congratulation. T. H. Robinson says the Aramaic phrase behind the Gospel words is an exclamation—'O the blessedness of . . .'. Martin Dibelius[2] translates, 'Hail you that are poor—for yours is the Kingdom of God', or 'Well is it with all the merciful, for mercy will be shown them'.

It does not seem possible to find any satisfactory substitute for the translation 'blessed', but we must take care to give the word the meaning of Jesus, which should become clearer as our study of the Beatitudes proceeds.[3]

2

The two versions of the Beatitudes in Matthew and Luke raise problems for the student. We cannot say definitely how the differences arose and the guesses of scholars are numerous and varied. There is not even agreement as to how many Beatitudes there are in Matthew. The usual reckoning

---

[1] *The Teachings of Jesus*, p. 247.

[2] *The Message of Jesus*, p. 62.

[3] It is interesting to note two other uses of the same Greek word in the N.T.: in John 13.17 where A.V. translates 'If ye know these things *happy* are ye if ye do them'; and in I Tim. 1.11, 'The glorious Gospel of the blessed God'. The happiness of the Christian God is in being a redeemer, comments Bruce in the *Expositor's Greek Testament*. See also Appendix for other Beatitudes in the Gospels p. 85.

is eight, but one scholar by taking verses 10, 11 and 12 separately makes the number ten, to balance the Decalogue. Some would exclude verses 10–12 from the reckoning altogether, on the ground that it is not a blessing upon character like the others, and so arrive at seven, the perfect number. Yet another scholar makes the total nine by counting separately the two uses of the word 'blessed' in what most people call the eighth Beatitude.

More important is the problem set by the disagreements between Matthew and Luke. While Matthew, on the usual reckoning, has eight Beatitudes, Luke has only four. But Luke has also four 'Woes', while Matthew has none. There are also differences in the actual wording of the Beatitudes which they do have in common, chiefly in the use by Luke of the second person, 'ye', and by his omission of words that in Matthew make clear the spiritual nature of the blessedness described. A detailed discussion of the many suggested explanations would be out of place here.[1]

Some of the difficulties, as will appear later, are more apparent than real. There is no reason why Jesus should not have used both forms. The vivid challenging statements in Luke seem characteristic of Him, but the longer forms in Matthew may represent His commentary and explanation. The first Beatitude in both Gospels can be shown to mean the same thing, despite the difference in language.[2] The Beatitudes were perhaps the 'Heads', which Jesus proceeded to elaborate and explain, and Matthew may have recorded more of the explanation than Luke. This would fit with Matthew's tendency as an editor. In his account of the Sermon on the Mount he has added to the main outline, as given by Luke from the document scholars call Q, other groups of sayings on similar topics, partly peculiar to himself, and partly to be found in other contexts in Luke. In verses 10-12 he seems to have put two versions of the

[1] See *Dictionary of Christ and the Gospels*, article 'Beatitude'.

[2] See pp. 28 ff.

same Beatitude side by side, or to have incorporated more comment than in the case of the others. We cannot rule out the possibility that Jesus spoke the Beatitudes on more than one occasion. If so, He might well, like other speakers, have used the same material clothed in different words.

In the selection of material for their Gospels the evangelists would inevitably be influenced by their own special concerns and interests. Like all of us, they found some of the teaching of Jesus more congenial and more intelligible than other parts. Largely unconsciously no doubt, they tended to select and stress what they understood, or thought they understood, and what had come home to them with greater force. This could readily be illustrated in detail from a comparison of the Gospels. Throughout we find Luke more radical, forceful, enthusiastic, a Gentile writing for Gentiles, where Matthew has an eye for Jewish readers. Apparently also each had access, in addition to common material, to separate strands of tradition. A full discussion would take us far beyond the proper sphere of this book. We must frankly acknowledge that we cannot fully account for the discrepancies in the versions.

Attempts to demonstrate a logical order in the Beatitudes are unconvincing and it is seldom that any two commentators agree. Our Lord is presenting different facets of the Christian character, not developing a line of thought. The Beatitudes describe not eight different people, but eight different characteristics of the true Christian. This is how the man in Christ should live; and will live so far as he is in Christ. Such a man is the citizen of the Kingdom of God, a man in whom God reigns. It is an attractive suggestion that 'for theirs is the Kingdom of heaven' may originally have been affixed as a refrain to each Beatitude, and not only to two as in our version.

The Beatitudes cannot be taken as providing a complete description of Christ's ideal character. There is much other supplementary teaching in the Gospels. Neither the Sermon on the Mount nor the Beatitudes is a systematic exposition.

3

What a startling reversal of the ordinary point of view the Beatitudes present. Ambrose called them 'the paradoxes of Christ'. They seem at first sight to offer 'a consolation prize for the defeated, a comfort for the heart-broken, a message for those who have failed in the struggle of life'.[1] Nietzsche said Christianity offered a 'slave morality'. Christianity is the religion of all poor devils, said some one else. Here, it seems, is Jesus offering comfort to the down-and-out, the beaten, the failures. Opponents of Christianity in the second century criticised it because it was a religion for the poor and the ignorant, for 'the very dregs of the population, peasants, mechanics, beggars and slaves'. Celsus invited people to judge the Church by the riff-raff it collected. Well, there would be nothing to be ashamed of in that: Jesus made no secret of inviting the weary and heavy-laden, the publican and the sinner. In reality, of course, the Beatitudes were spoken primarily to a group of vigorous young men whom Jesus was sending out to turn the world upside down. Though no doubt overheard by others, the Sermon on the Mount was addressed to the disciples (Matt. 5.1. and Luke 6.20. Luke pictures three concentric rings, the twelve, the disciples, the multitude. Luke 6.13-20). This is not a message for men in general. It only makes sense in the setting of Jesus' teaching about God and His Kingdom. Only men of such a spirit, of endurance and courage, can hope to perform the tasks to which He is calling His followers. Was it even perhaps a kind of Gideon's test to weed out the hesitant? 'The ethical teaching of Jesus', wrote a great Jewish scholar, C. G. Montefiore, 'is an ethical teaching for heroes.'[2]

Although many of the Beatitudes are Old Testament echoes and parallels to several of them can be found in

[1] James Reid, *The Key to the Kingdom*, p. 13. This is the most helpful discussion of the Beatitudes known to me and I have quoted it several times in this book.

[2] *The Old Testament and After*, p. 241.

contemporary Jewish literature, the contrast with typical Judaism is striking. The Old Testament standards of blessedness are often material, an honourable, upright worldly prosperity—long life, cattle, crops, wealth, descendants (e.g. the 'beatitudes' of Deut. 33 and 28, Job 42.10-17). This picture of the true citizen of God's Kingdom is in striking contrast also to the popular dreams of a political rebirth of the nation and of a Kingdom of God erected on the necks of the conquered Roman oppressors. To the enthusiastic revolutionary the Beatitudes would come like a dash of cold water. There is the same contrast with the ideals of other religions. For example, one of the Chinese Classics, *The Book of History*, has a list of the Five Happinesses—long life, riches, soundness of body and serenity of mind, love of virtue, and an end crowning the life; not at all a bad list, and yet how different from the outlook of the Beatitudes.

But the Beatitudes are no less, indeed more, in contrast with the ideals of the average modern. If a man is to 'get on', he needs an assertive spirit, a clever, calculating mind, feelings that are not too sensitive to the misfortunes of others, self-confidence, and the art of self-advertisement. If you want happiness, many a man today would say, you must grab all the money you can get, avoid pain and suffering, don't be too squeamish about people who get in your way, stand up for your rights, assert yourself. He finds something inhuman in the Beatitudes, weak, unworthy of red-blooded men; an impossible dream, and not even a pleasant one.

Perhaps in some quarters there is a little less assurance in this revolt against the Christian ethic. 'We used to be told that people would be happy so soon as they could get free from inhibitions, from the artificial moral repressions that the old moral laws imposed upon them; now they have freed themselves amazingly, and with increasing speed, but are they happy?'[1] That is why Jesus sighs over the rich, the satisfied, the thoughtlessly gay, the popular. The 'Woe to'

[1] Rosalind Murray, *The Good Pagan's Failure*, p. 61.

of the Authorised Version would be better translated 'Alas for'. It is a lament, not an expression of ill-will, or even of judgment, except a judgment of fact, of insight into the real state of affairs; Jesus was sorry for such people because they were likely to despise the true riches He offered. Power, wealth, the quest for pleasure and popularity, are not true paths to happiness. Beatrice in *Purgatorio* tells of how Dante, after her death, 'turned his steps down a way which was no true path, following false phantoms of delight, which keep no promises they make to man'. Jesus came that He might bring men fulness of life and free them from the crippling and degradation that are the fruit of sin. The Beatitudes were addressed to men who knew that, who had heard from His lips 'words of eternal life' and had experienced His transforming power.

In trying to understand the Beatitudes we must never forget that original audience. They were Jews as well as followers of Jesus. They accepted and revered the teaching of the Old Testament. Jesus too revered it, though He often corrected, qualified or supplemented it. The Old Testament was there in the minds of His hearers and unless He said otherwise we ought to assume that He used the words in their Old Testament sense. He has often been misunderstood because men have forgotten that.

We must remember also that Jesus spoke first to His audience and not to us. Instructions to His disciples how to behave on a missionary journey are obviously not regulations for home life in modern Britain, but even the Beatitudes must be understood in the light of the historical situation and the association of words and ideas for the immediate hearers. They have undying value for us and for all generations, but only if we take pains first to understand what they meant to those who heard them. All this seems very obvious, yet it is ignored every day, both by those who would find in the Sermon on the Mount literal legislation for today, and by those who dismiss it as of no relevance to our needs. We shall be wise not to be content with surface meanings.

The words have a history and a background; and they must be read in the light of the rest of our Lord's teaching.

4

The Beatitudes are not the substitution of the second commandment of love for one's neighbour for the first of love for God. The extraordinary notion that the Sermon on the Mount contains simple moral precepts detached from theological complications, could surely not survive one attentive reading of it. It is full of theological presuppositions. In the Christian scheme of things, and in reality, love of the Father and love of His children are not to be separated. In chillier language, religion and ethics belong together. In the end of the day you cannot have the one without the other. 'To be "good",' it has been said, 'is not the same as to be Christian although being Christian should include being "good".'[1] The Beatitudes are not moral precepts but the revelation of the blessedness of a new way of life in reliance upon our Father in heaven. They are vitally dependent upon Jesus' teaching about the nature of God and what He has done for men; on the other hand, God's redemption in Christ calls imperatively for a new kind of behaviour between man and man (Matt. 7.16-23; Luke 6.46; I John 4.7-21).

The enlightened humanist often claims to accept 'the Christian ethic' detached from what he regards as its super-added, irrelevant doctrinal beliefs. And in such 'good pagans', to use Rosalind Murray's phrase, are often to be found eagerness to grapple with injustice, sympathy, much kindliness. Humanists are not 'bad' while Christians are 'good'. The problem is not so easy as that. And if humanists are often better than their creed, nominal Christians are unhappily often worse than theirs.

The humanist's valuation of life is marred by his refusal, or inability, to see it against the background of eternity and a future life. His perspective ends at the graveside. He is

[1] Murray, *op. cit.*, p. 72.

apt, too, to measure himself against an attainable ideal of a balanced, cultured life governed by a sense of honour, duty and self-respect. It is a fine ideal and its exponents are often charming people and admirable citizens. 'The Christian, on the other hand, measures himself by quite another standard, not in human excellence, but in relation to God. He is a citizen of another city. . . . He is living his life as it were in a new dimension, in which the goodness he has attained seems negligible, non-existent, in comparison to the goodness he apprehends.'[1] Of the Christian's unattainable ideal we shall have more to say later (p. 21).

While in this country the doctrines of Christianity have lost much of their authority, yet lip-service is widely paid to Christian ethics and they are still to some extent genuinely accepted as a guide to conduct. But it is becoming clearer that ethics are in fact bound up with faith. The fading of a real belief in God has gone along with a slackening of moral restraint. Non-Christian values are widely and unquestioningly accepted today even by nominal Christians. To use an illustration of William Temple, the world is like a shop window in which some practical joker has moved all the price tickets round, so that valueless things have high prices set on them, and things of great value are rated low.

More than he realises the humanist is living on borrowed capital. He has derived his standards of value from a faith he has discarded. A slip coach goes on running after it has been detached from the train, and cut flowers remain beautiful. You can find men who have repudiated Christian belief who are shining examples of Christian conduct. But if we want a continuous supply of flowers we must look to the garden, and carriages without engines don't go far. If the Christian God is denied, Christian moral standards will not long survive.

Many readers of the Gospels are disturbed by their apparent remoteness from present-day life. Most of our modern moral perplexities are not even mentioned. The most

[1] Murray, *op. cit.*, p. 31.

diligent use of a concordance will not find answers to our
problems. The distinctively Christian message is in terms of
persons, not of social systems and political programmes.
This does not mean that Christian discipleship cannot
influence and transform systems and programmes; it has
done so and can do so again. But the Church can seldom
usefully act on the social order corporately, from outside.
Its task is to bring society back from false perverted values
and aims. 'The really important changes can be effected only
from within. The conduct of public life, of administration,
and of industry, involves a multitude of decisions from day
to day by countless individuals, and there can be no deep
change except by the progressive transformation of the
insights and motives which prompt these decisions.'[1]

Jesus is not concerned to give mankind a new code of
rules for detailed behaviour, but to commend to men by
His words and by His example the way of love, of sincere
goodwill, in the relations between man and man. To Him
that was the sum of all the commandments, the sovereign
remedy for all troubles, the one way in which to face one's
fellows, be they friends or enemies, our family circle or the
stranger fallen among thieves, the hungry, the sick, the
prisoner. Follow love through to the end, He says. . . . But
how few of us have succeeded, or even tried.

He revealed all this not as the supreme moral Teacher,
but as man's Saviour, as the Word made flesh. It is love
embodied in His life and death and not only in His Beatitudes that has won men's allegiance. The foundation of
Christianity is not a system of doctrine or code of morals,
or a Sermon, but a Person.[2]

So understood the Beatitudes are more searching than
the Decalogue. Part of the point of the Sermon on the
Mount is the contrast between God's real will for men and

[1] *The Churches Survey Their Task*. Edited by J. H. Oldham, p. 45.

[2] There is an admirable chapter on 'Religion and Morals' in *The
Teaching of Jesus* by T. W. Manson.

the rules of the Law, revealed to be inadequate and superficial. When Isaiah saw the Lord he saw his own sinfulness.
If we begin to see the meaning of the Beatitudes we realise
how far short we have come of Christ's way of life. By God's
standards there is none good—no (Rom. 3.9ff.), not one.

And we may well find the Beatitudes as great a stumbling
block as any article of the creed. The presuppositions and
assumptions of our generation, and our own personal
prejudices and preferences, our own ambitions, may be the
greatest of all hindrances to our entering Christ's Kingdom.
'A man may believe in the Nicene Creed or in the creed
attributed to Athanasius or in the Confession of Augsburg
or the Confession of the Westminster Divines, but if he
does not believe in the Sermon on the Mount—believe in
it seriously as containing the laws which must govern his
own life—he has denied the faith and is in revolt against
Christ. The doctrine and the ethics of the Christian revelation are really inseparable.'[1] Much is said by people who
shrink from the theological implications of the New
Testament about their admiration for the Beatitudes. It
would be harsh to say that they were insincere, but they are
certainly thoughtless. Even if we forget that they imply
the theology, what a stern test they present to any man who
would try to live them out.

5

The main characteristics of the way of life set out in the
Beatitudes may perhaps be summarised under four
headings.

(a) *Inwardness*. 'Inwardness, rightness of heart or spirit,
is the special and pre-eminent characteristic of Christian
goodness.'[2] This is clearly enunciated throughout the
Sermon. The Christian is to be free from hate as well as
from committing murder. He is to flee lustful thoughts as

[1] Dale, *Laws of Christ for Common Life*, p. 215.

[2] Sidgwick, *History of Ethics*, p. 114.

well as adultery. He is to rid himself of insincerity in all
his words and not only to refrain from perjury. Character,
goodness of heart, is more fundamental than good deeds;
the good deeds reveal the good man behind them. The
citizens of the Kingdom are the kind of people to whom in
their fellowship with God it is possible and natural to do
the right things. From within out of the heart of man spring
good and evil. Nothing more searching has ever been spoken
in the realm of ethics than the words of Jesus: 'Every good
tree bringeth forth good fruit, but a corrupt tree bringeth
forth evil fruit. A good tree cannot bring forth evil fruit,
neither can a corrupt tree bring forth good fruit.' (Matt.
7.17-18.)

(b) *Enthusiasm, earnestness, perseverance.* The stress laid
on spirit and character is not to the exclusion of action. It
is not the peace lover but the peace maker who is blessed.
The desire to injure is wrong even if not converted into
action; to regard another merely as an object of lust is the
same kind of sin as adultery. Yet the tree is known by its
fruits, (Matt. 7.20) and the end of the Sermon praises the
man who *acts* upon the teaching and not the man who
merely hears it with approval (Matt. 7.24-27). To wish to
do good is splendid. It is essential. But to stop at the wish is
not enough. Evil desires which shrink from action are still evil,
but good desires which do not express themselves in action
when they can, are only half good. There is a saying
attributed to Jesus in the fragment of Irenaeus' letter to
Victor: When a man is able to do good and does not do it,
he is alien from the love of God (cf. Matt. 7.21).

(c) *Detachment from the world's prizes and honours* for the
sake of allegiance to Christ. 'Ye know that the princes of
the Gentiles exercise dominion over them, and they that are
great exercise authority upon them. But it shall not be so
among you . . .' (Matt. 20.25-28).

(d) *Love, not self-regard.* It is possible to do the right
deed in the wrong way, so that the same action may be a
benediction or an insult. Paul knew those who were ready

to give their bodies to be burned, but without love. That great Indian Christian, afterwards to become Bishop Azariah of Dornakal, moved the World Missionary Conference at Edinburgh in 1910 by his appeal. He spoke with gratitude for the devoted labours and self-sacrifice of the missionaries. 'You have given us so much. Give us one thing more. Give us friends.'

That these characteristics do underly the way of the Beatitudes we shall see more clearly as the book proceeds.

6

But surely all this is equivalent to saying that the Beatitudes present us with an unattainable, useless, impracticable ideal? Unattainable, yes; but not therefore useless or impracticable. The great artist—and the greater he is the more he feels it—never attains his ideal. He never quite transfers all he sees to the canvas. Something eludes him. He is always learning and trying. Art has an unattainable goal: that is the spur and inspiration of the artist. It lures him on.

Jesus does not present us with a rule of behaviour which common-sense will immediately endorse. He startles. He challenges accepted standards and values, creates aspiration, longing, discontent. He makes an inexorable demand for the impossible: 'Ye shall be perfect as your heavenly Father is perfect.' We must be content with nothing less than that. And so we shall never be content. The greater the saint the more conscious he is of coming short. Paul counted himself not to have attained the prize of the upward calling of God in Christ Jesus (Phil. 3.12-14, R.V. margin).

The real question about any man is not so much what he has achieved as what he is aiming at; what he is trying to be; what he reveres. 'The beginning is right reverence not right resolve, because above every other test of us, what we are able to honour is, in our deepest hearts, what we are, and in our ultimate attainment what we shall be. The supreme

hindrance to the coming of God's Kingdom is idolatry not
evil doing.'[1] We worship the wrong gods.

The unattainable ideal stirs perpetual effort to respond to
its demands. It is only when we think of it as a regulation or
law laying down precise action for particular cases that it
becomes inhibiting or useless. What the Christian must do
is to respond to his utmost to the demand of God's love
upon him in the particular situation. God's love for us and
at the same time for our neighbours make upon us a demand
which we can never fully satisfy and which therefore leaves
in us no room for complacency. Of course, our reach
must exceed our grasp. We need a standard, a criticism, a
spur.

An interesting and instructive commentary on this may be
found in Julian Huxley's comparison of the effects of Islam
and Christianity on African life. 'Wherever Islam has made
headway in Africa, it has led to a definite and real progress,
but to a progress which has then been arrested. Christianity
even in cases where it is strictest in the matter of rules of
life, ritual or credal efficacy does invariably insist on the
importance of the inner life and of high standards in
regard to it. The standards of Christianity are often described as impracticable and impossible, leading inevitably
to hypocrisy or a divorce between precept and practice.
This may be true in its degree, yet it seems undoubted that
it is the very impossibility for the Christian of living up to
the standard of his religion which has given Christianity its
real vitality. It is impossible to live up to any standard of
perfection in matters intellectual or artistic as well as ethical.
But the fact that it is cherished impels to further effort.'[2]

7

Another criticism often offered of the Christian ethic, and
of the Beatitudes in particular, is that they are based upon

[1] John Oman, *Grace and Personality*, p. 78.
[2] Africa View. 1931.

the lure of reward, in the next world if not in this. At first
sight there seems some justification for the criticism. Jesus
does speak of rewards. 'Love your enemies . . . and your
reward shall be great' (Luke 6.35). 'Thy Father which seeth
in secret shall reward thee.' (Matt. 6.4. The word 'openly' is
probably not in the original. See R.V.) 'Whosoever shall
give to drink a cup of cold water only . . . he shall in no
wise lose his reward' (Matt. 10.42; Luke 18.28-30; Matt.
19.21). And each of the Beatitudes has a promise, if not a
reward, attached to it. Do the Beatitudes in fact encourage a
response to selfish motives? Or is Jesus emphasising what
Fosdick has called 'the rebound of blessing on the good
man's life', the result that follows, not the motive that
inspires?

Note, first, that Jesus constantly criticised good acts,
almsgiving or prayer, done for selfish motives to gain
applause or reward, in the very same context in which He is
apparently offering rewards. That should make us think
again as to His real meaning (cf. Matt. 6.1-6; Luke 6.32-36,
14.12-14; Matt. 5.5. or Mark 10.30, if literal, would con-
tradict Mark 8.34-37; Luke 9.57-58).

Again, if you are good *in order to* inherit the Kingdom of
God, you are not being good at all. You are not generous if
you are giving in order to be 'repaid a thousandfold'. Sir
Thomas Browne said that fear of hell had not made him
seek good, nor did he think it would make any man. 'I fear
God, yet am not afraid of Him; His mercies make me
ashamed of my sins, before His judgments afraid thereof . . .
I hardly think there was ever any scared into heaven: they
go the fairest way to heaven that would serve God without a
hell.' Caswall's translation of the poem attributed to St.
Francis Xavier is in many of our hymnbooks:

> My God, I love Thee; not because
> I hope for heaven thereby,
> Nor yet because who love thee not
> Are lost eternally. . . .

Not with the hope of gaining aught;
　　Not seeking a reward;
But as Thyself hast loved me,
　　O ever loving Lord.

Even so I love Thee, and will love,
　　And in Thy praise will sing,
Solely because Thou art my God
　　And my eternal King

Man *cannot* be good for fear of the consequences or for hope of a reward.

Further, it is God's approval Jesus bids us seek, and not man's. No pretence can deceive Him. It is no use acting goodness because it is going to pay you. He sees the heart (cf. I Cor. 13.3).

Neither here nor elsewhere is Jesus teaching that we have any *claims* to a reward. In His grace God gives out of all proportion to services rendered. We cannot put God in our debt. At best, we are servants. We have but done our duty (Luke 17.10).

All this becomes still more clear when we look at the nature of the 'rewards'. If you hunger for righteousness, righteousness will be your reward: not gold or fame or long life. 'In the Kingdom of God service is not a stepping stone to nobility: it *is* nobility, the only kind of nobility that is recognised.'[1] When we are urged to lay up treasure in heaven, there is no promise that men will receive there the things men treasure in this life, as apparently in the Muhammadan paradise. The treasures of heaven are spiritual. Loyalty in service does receive recompense; it is the citizenship of the Kingdom of God, which can make no appeal except to those who seek first the Kingdom in goodness and unselfishness. The 'rewards' are of like quality to the virtues.

And we must not forget the last Beatitude. 'Verily I say

[1] T W. Manson, *The Church's Ministry*, p. 27.

unto you', said Jesus at another time, 'There is no man that hath left house, or brethren, or sisters, or father, or mother, or wife, or children, or lands for my sake and the gospel's, but he shall receive an hundredfold now in this time, houses, and brethren, and sisters, and mothers, and children, and lands, *with persecutions*; and in the world to come eternal life' (Mark 10.28-31). Obviously literalism is out of place here, and there is more than a touch of irony or humour in Jesus' reply. Yet it is true that the man who leaves home and family for Christ's service enters a wider family and finds stronger ties of love. Christ's promises are not arbitrary bribes but the natural fruition of a good life. The 'rewards' are not material rewards, but are such as to appeal only to the devoted and unselfish servant; the Christian is always entering into his Lord's joy: that is his reward here and hereafter, not a payment. The rewards are promised only to those who act not for the sake of the rewards, but for the sake of the Kingdom. It is another of the characteristic paradoxes of Jesus. He that saves his life loses it; he that loses finds.

Yet there is more to be said, if by 'reward' is meant the assurance that in the end of the day it will be well with the righteous, that trust in God is not misplaced, that there is ultimate victory for the righteousness for which the Christian must stand here and now in scorn of consequence, and that in that victory the loyal will have their part. 'Though it is essential that an action, to be truly moral, should not be performed for the sake of its consequences . . . yet to deny that in the discharge of duty ultimate satisfaction can be found and the best capacities of the self realised, is to leave the mind which acquiesces in such a denial a bewildered waif in an incoherent and irrational world.'[1] Religion stands not only for the doing of one's duty, but also for the faith that in doing it we are in league with the universe, obeying God the Father Almighty. The righteousness Christ would have us hunger for is the true food of our spirits.

[1] Clement Webb, *The Contribution of Christianity to Ethics*, p. 70.

It is the Creator's righteousness. Duty is the 'stern daughter of the voice of God'. Christian faith is trust 'that conscience will prove no lying voice, and love and selfless service no blind guides to the ultimate meaning of the giant system of things in which we find ourselves involved'.[1]

8

One more general introductory point remains to be made, but it is of the first importance. We misunderstand the Christian Faith altogether if we think of it as primarily a moral demand upon us. As we have seen, the moral demand upon the Christian is inescapable, but the Gospel is first and foremost not the presentation of an ideal of human conduct. It is the proclamation of what God has done for men. The Gospel is not exhortation or good advice or rules to be observed at one's peril. It is the power of God unto salvation. John Wesley's story cannot be retold too often. Like Paul and Luther before him he tried to find redemption through morality. He sought to earn salvation by good deeds. The Moravians helped to move him from his legal and self-righteous religion but it was not till he went 'very unwillingly' to a meeting in Aldersgate Street on Wednesday, May 24th, 1738, that he really understood. Someone was reading Luther's preface to the Epistle to the Romans, and as he heard Luther's interpretation of Paul's experience, and recognised his own plight, he felt his heart 'strangely warmed'. By 'trust in Christ, Christ alone, for salvation' he entered a new world. He had been a servant, now he became a son in his Father's house. He knew we were saved by grace, by God's undeserved goodness to us, and not by our own achievements. (The story should be read in full in Wesley's *Journal*.)

The real saints are happy folk—almost irresponsible they seem to the outsider. They are very much in earnest, but they are not staggering like some Atlas under 'the heavy and the weary weight of all this unintelligible world'.

[1] John Baillie, *The Roots of Religion*, p. 127.

John Baillie[1] recalls a story Spurgeon told 'about one of his fellow ministers who went to the house of a poor old woman with a contribution of money for the payment of her rent. He knocked again and again but failed to get any response. Nevertheless the old woman was all the time within, and her explanation afterwards was "I heard the knocking but I thought it was the man come to ask for the rent".' 'He who stands at the door,' adds Baillie, 'has come with a gift, but we are so ready to think He has come for payment. The knock is a Saviour's knock, but we are so ready to think it a Taskmaster's.'

---

[1] *Invitation to Pilgrimage*, p. 48.

II

Blessed are the poor in spirit: for theirs is the Kingdom
of heaven. Matt. 5.3.
Blessed are ye poor: for yours is the Kingdom of God.
Luke 6.20.

THE difference in wording between the versions of Matthew
and Luke has given rise to much discussion. Luke apparently
records a blessing upon an external condition, while
Matthew is concerned with a condition of inner character.
Probably Luke's form is nearer to what Jesus actually said,
but it is also likely that Matthew's words represent more
accurately to the modern reader the meaning of the saying
and what it would convey to those who first heard the
words. In Jewish writings of the time of Christ 'poor' was
practically equivalent to 'faithful believers', and had lost
almost entirely any reference to material poverty. The usage
points back to the days of persecution when the poor were
more faithful to their religion than the rich who often
became contaminated with paganism in thought and life.
With psalmists and prophets 'rich' tends to mean worldly
and 'poor' to mean religious.[1] In Luke the Beatitude is
addressed to the disciples: 'ye poor'. Properly understood
both versions mean the same thing, and whatever His
precise wording, there is little doubt that to the audience of
Jesus the religious associations of the word would be
uppermost.

It is of course true that Christianity has been a Gospel
to the poor in material goods. Perhaps Jesus was insisting
that poverty is no bar to the Kingdom of God as it is to so
many good things of this world. He can hardly have meant
that poverty in itself is a blessing or that only poor people

---

[1] See, e.g., Isa. 61.1, R.V. margin, 66.2; Ps. 9.9-12, 10.2, 12, 69.29,
72.2, 86.1-2. In the Psalms of Solomon, almost contemporary with the
N.T., the 'sinners' are rich and prosperous, and the 'saints' are poor.

can enter the Kingdom of God. To suppose that would be to run counter to all His other teaching and to His dealings with wealthy people. Jesus knew how poverty may turn life into a mere struggle for existence. 'He would have been the last', says James Reid, 'to fling a text to a starving man and comfort him with the suggestion of spiritual riches.' He cared if men were hungry and ill-clad (e.g. Matt. 25.31-46). Jesus showed no hatred of the rich as such and He certainly did not make poverty a general condition of discipleship. The rich young ruler was a special case (Luke 18.18-25). There have, of course, been movements in the history of the Church which have read His teaching otherwise, and individuals like St. Francis of Assisi who believed that Christian discipleship called them to poverty.

Yet we must not forget, especially because it is contrary to our cherished beliefs, that one of the outstanding features of the teaching of Jesus is His emphasis on the danger of being rich. Covetousness is one of the greatest of sins in His eyes. He is much sterner in His judgment upon greediness than upon others more sternly condemned by most of us. He insists constantly on the deceitfulness of riches, (Matt. 13.22) and tells us that so far from its being easier for a rich man to be religious than for a poor one (as most of us really believe) it is in fact only by a miracle that a rich man can get into the Kingdom of God at all (Matt. 19.23-26). The wealthy man accustomed to finding all doors fly open at the sight of his money stands at the gate of the Kingdom as helpless and ridiculous as a camel, wondering how he is going to thread his way through the eye of a needle. J. D. Rockefeller declared: 'The poorest man I know is the man who has nothing but money', and certainly some of the wealthiest men I have known have had very little in the bank. 'A man's life consisteth not in the abundance of the things that he possesseth' (Luke 12.15). So St. Paul claimed to be 'a pauper, yet a means of blessing to many; without a penny yet possessing all things' (II Cor. 6.10. Translation by Newton Davies in the *Abingdon Commentary*).

So it would not be surprising to find Jesus in this Beatitude telling the poor that they might really be better off than the rich, if only they knew it. Wealth *can* be handled in a Christian way, but it is very difficult. Great extremes of wealth are apt to poison human relations, and rich men are apt to dominate more than they should in church and state. Success and prosperity tend to lead men to be self satisfied and arrogant. In nothing is the attitude of Jesus more different from that of men in general than in the fact that He is sorry for rich people because of the perils and difficulties of their position. Is there anything upon which men are more agreed than in regarding the amassing of material goods and the increase of wealth as the true ends of living? The teaching of Jesus is in sharp contradiction to all that.

But we certainly must not imagine that Jesus believed that hunger and want were good things, or that He would look with an approving eye on the compulsory, grinding poverty that makes life for many in the modern world so dreary, if not an actual struggle for survival. Poverty may degrade no less than wealth. Jesus does not teach a sentimental pose of superiority to money and all that money stands for. Life itself and the decencies and pleasures of living for ourselves and our families are dependent upon our having an adequate amount of money. I find nothing in the teaching of our Lord that suggests that we should pretend to be indifferent to such considerations: still less that we should think them un-important for other people. It is the *love* of money that is a root of all kinds of evil (I Tim. 6.10, R.V.)—not necessarily its possession. We may be in no danger of being rich, yet we may be covetous and have the love of money in our hearts, and the rich man may not.

If the reference here is to material poverty at all, which is doubtful, it is probably a blessing upon those who are not possessed by their possessions, as the rich fool was (Luke 12.16-21). It might well be a commendation of people who are ready, if the service of the Kingdom demands it, to be

poor in material wealth as they already are poor in heart;
free from the tyranny of covetousness, the disease of ac-
quisitiveness, unencumbered and free to follow.

But I suspect that Jesus was not thinking of cash and
goods at all. 'Poor in spirit'—what does that mean? Certainly not poor-spirited, a dejected, self-pitying creature
without any backbone or 'stuffing'.

I believe Jesus means the opposite of all that is summed up
in the word 'pride', which heads Dante's list of the seven
deadly sins. The poor in spirit is the man who does not boast
of his talents or attainments, because he knows he has
nothing that he did not receive. If he is 'gifted', as we
significantly say, it is because he has been given much. He is
humble about his own character because he sees it in the
light that comes from Jesus. He knows he has nothing to
be conceited about. He knows that in his own soul are the
possibilities or the actualities of the sins that put Jesus on the
cross. If he has made progress in the Christian life it is all
due to the grace of God. He knows how far short he comes
and how great is his need. The poor in spirit are the antithesis of the proud, the spiritually well-fed and satisfied
and complacent. 'Blessed are those who feel their spiritual
need' is Goodspeed's translation.

In the Book of the Revelation is the description of the
Church at Laodicea. It was a prosperous, fashionable
church, well satisfied with itself. 'I am rich', it said, 'and
have gotten riches and have need of nothing', and did not
know that in fact and in the sight of God it was wretched
and miserable and poor and naked (Rev. 3.14-22). It was
so rich in spirit and so proud, that it had no room for
God.

> If thou could'st empty all thyself of self
> Like to a shell dishabited,
> Then would He find thee on the ocean shelf
> And say: This is not dead,
> And fill thee with Himself instead.

But thou art so replete with very thou
That when He comes He saith: This is enow
Unto itself. Twere better let it be.
It is so small and full. There is no room for Me.

(T. E. BROWN.)

The wealthy in spirit are sure they can get along quite well without God and see no Gospel in Christianity. Pride is a declaration of independence of God. Jesus declared that the one hopeless condition was when a man was satisfied with himself and sure that there was nothing wrong with *him*. The story of the pharisee and the publican asserts that it is better to be a sinner and know it, than to be a so-called good man who does not recognise the evil in his own heart. God can do nothing with a self-righteous and self-satisfied man.

On the tombstone of William Carey at Serampore you may read the inscription set there by his own instructions. There is the name, with no honours or degrees, the dates 1761-1834, and then a quotation from a now forgotten hymn by Isaac Watts,

> A wretched, poor and helpless worm
> On thy kind arms I fall.

There is nothing more. We do not talk like that today, and the language may even strike us as rather funny, but we can surely appreciate the spirit of the very great and learned man who chose that for his epitaph. 'If God could use me', he once said, 'he can use anybody.'

To be poor in spirit is to see ourselves truly, as we are in the sight of God, and to be awake to our need of His love and forgiveness. It means an entire absence of conceit and self-sufficiency. How few of us are within sight of that. But that is to be as all the great saints have been and to be able to receive the divine bounty. We can make no claim upon God because of our worthiness. We approach Him with empty hands to receive a love we can never earn and yet which is ours for the taking.

'Blessed are the poor in spirit: for theirs is the Kingdom of heaven.' *Theirs* is emphatic in the Greek. There is no difference in meaning between Matthew's Kingdom of heaven and Luke's Kingdom of God. It was a common practice of Jewish writers from motives of reverence to use substitutes for the name of God.

The Kingdom means no glorified Welfare State, but the realm in which God rules, where the Father's name is hallowed and men behave as His children. The poor in spirit are those over whom God rules. They are true citizens of the Kingdom. They are at home in God's family. And there can be no greater blessedness than that. It *is* theirs: here and now, not only in the next world. Wherever a human heart is devoted to God's service there the Kingdom is present. The Kingdom can only fully come in heaven, but even here men may enrol as its citizens and enjoy many of the privileges of citizenship.

In the *Purgatorio*, where, in Dante's thought, men are purged of their sins and prepared for entrance to Paradise, pride must be conquered on the lowest terrace of all. For until pride is overcome the soul cannot hope to mount higher. As Dante leaves the terrace he hears voices chanting this Beatitude: 'Blessed are the poor in spirit.'

The numerous attempts that have been made to find a meaning in the order of the Beatitudes are unconvincing. Yet we can agree that it is fitting that the blessing on the poor in spirit should come first. Dante was right. This is the necessary foundation for the Christian character.

> Nothing in my hand I bring;
> Simply to Thy cross I cling;
> Naked, come to Thee for dress;
> Helpless, look to Thee for grace.
> Foul, I to the fountain fly.
>   Wash me, Saviour, or I die.

There is fundamental Christianity in these old familiar words.

III

> Blessed are they that mourn: for they shall be comforted.
> Matt. 5.4.
> Blessed are ye that weep now: for ye shall laugh. Luke
> 6.21.

'NEVER man spake like this man'. We do not know what evoked that verdict. Perhaps it was the note of authority in His voice, or the force and appeal of His personality. But perhaps it was the startling and unexpected things that He said. Who else would have said: 'Blessed are the mourners for they shall be comforted'?

Is it really true? we ask ourselves. If experience teaches anything, surely it is a fact that sorrow is not always a blessing. It may embitter and harden. Nor is sorrow always sure of comfort. Men and women have died of a broken heart, or nursed their grief to their life's end. Here, as so often with Christ's teaching, we must probe beneath the surface meaning to understand what He is really saying to us. He put His teachings in such arresting and puzzling ways to startle us awake and make us think. That is one reason for His parables.

Just as it is not always blessed to be poor, so blessing and comfort do not come to all mourners. No condition of life is necessarily and universally blessed. Perhaps as many people are made worse by sorrow as are made better, in spite of all that poets and religious teachers have written about its purifying and sweetening influences.

The Beatitudes were spoken to Christ's disciples and it is only for those who face sorrow in Christ's way that comfort is assured. For them, as James Reid has written, there is 'an alchemy of the spirit whereby the hard and bitter stuff of experience is changed, here and now, into the very nourishment of the soul'.[1] For those who reject or ignore or have never heard of the love of God, mourning may breed only cynicism and despair. Christians are not blessed because

[1] *Op. cit.*, p. 63.

they mourn but because in their sorrow they find comfort in the love of God. The word 'mourning' means bereavement to us today, but this assurance covers all trouble and distress. Death is not the worst evil that can befall a family. There are broken homes where husband or wife has been unfaithful, or where fathers and mothers are distressed beyond telling by the way of life of son or daughter. Christ does not ask us to pretend that we are not hurt or that sorrow and disaster are not real.

How do men seek to offer comfort to the mourner? Think of the happiness you have had, they say: it is better to have loved and lost than never to have loved at all. That is true and no doubt it helps. Or they advise people to seek distraction from their grief by finding other interests, by amusement, by travel. And no doubt that is wise. Or they assure them that life's sorrows and injustices will be put right in the next world. Or that it is the will of God and must be accepted—often substituting fatalism for Christian faith, since many of life's disasters come from human folly and sin, and not from God at all. Or we assure ourselves and others that suffering and bereavement are the common lot of man and must just be accepted. There is a story that a woman appealed to the Buddha for the restoration of her dead child. He promised to grant her request if she would bring him at nightfall a bowl full of peppercorns collected from homes in which the family circle was complete—in which father, mother, husband, wife, son, daughter, were all there. The woman set off with high hopes. But she returned at night fall with an empty bowl. This again is well to remember. But Buddha and the Stoics do not help us much. 'Vacant chaff well meant for grain', Tennyson called such comfort for the loss of his friend, Hallam.

> That loss is common would not make
> My own less bitter, rather more:
> Too common! Never morning wore
> To evening, but some heart did break.

All this, says H. H. Farmer, is 'the worldly wisdom of comfort. It is to be found in all the pagan moralists and writers'.[1] Such ways of facing sorrow have their value. They are good so far as they go, but they are not the Christian way.

Christ assures us that it is well with those who die in Him. They rest from their labours, and their works do follow them. We may grieve for our own loss but not for them. Death is no disaster for those who die in Christ. They have gone to their Father's home, and the time of reunion will come. To be sure of that does bring comfort.

Also to those who open their hearts to the love of God there comes in time of need a healing Presence of understanding sympathy. He bindeth up the broken hearted.

But I believe Christ has yet more to say to the mourner.

Our sorrow is born of our love, and when it is carried with the aid of Christ our love will grow by reason of our sorrow and will draw others into its circle. It will help us to help others. 'Blessed be God', says St. Paul, who had learned this lesson, 'even the Father of our Lord Jesus Christ, the Father of mercies, and the God of all comfort; who comforteth us in all our tribulation, that we may be able to comfort them which are in any trouble, by the comfort wherewith we ourselves are comforted of God. For as the sufferings of Christ abound in us, so our consolation also aboundeth by Christ' (II. Cor. 1.3-5). 'The sufferings of Christ' were willingly accepted by Him in taking up the burden of men's need. To accept our suffering in like manner, to follow so in His steps in our measure is to find our own burden lighter. We fill up, Paul dares to say, what is lacking in the sufferings of Christ (Col. 1.24).

John Bright lost his wife after less than two years of happy married life. She died in radiant Christian faith. 'It seemed not like the chamber of death', he wrote later. 'There was nothing fearful in that memorable time—it was more as the gate of Heaven.' Yet Bright was, in his own

[1] *The Healing Cross*, p. 135.

words, 'in the depths of grief, I might almost say of despair'. His friend Cobden called to see him, bringing not only deep sympathy, but a summons. Bright told the story many years later at the unveiling of Cobden's statue in Bradford. 'After a time he (Cobden) looked up and said, "There are thousands of houses in England at this moment where wives, mothers and children are dying of hunger. Now", he said, "when the first paroxysm of your grief is past, I would advise you to come with me, and we will never rest till the Corn Law is repealed".' And to that appeal Bright responded with results which history records.[1] That way of mourning, which turns it into sympathy for the grief and needs of others, finds comfort. We are not Brights or Cobdens but we can let our sufferings and sorrows teach us sympathy.

Here, indeed, I believe may be the clue to the deeper meaning of this Beatitude. I think it goes beyond the offer of comfort to those facing personal bereavement. It is a blessing upon those who mourn for the needs of others, whose hearts are full of sympathy for their fellows. 'The saddest thing in all God's world', writes James Reid, 'is not a soul that sorrows: it is a heart so dull that it is incapable of feeling grief at all; a heart so selfish that nothing but what touches its comfort and its ease could move it to a twinge of feeling. For to sorrow means to love. Mourning is indeed but another and a deeper side of loving.'[2]

The blessing of this Beatitude is for those who for Christ's sake refuse to shield their hearts from the griefs and pains of others, who feel the whip that is laid on the shoulders of another man, who might be sheltered but who choose to face the storm that they may lend a helping hand to those who are caught in its fury. Moses refusing to be called the son of Pharaoh's daughter and sharing the lot of his oppressed people, was a mourner in this sense. It is the very heart of the missionary motive. To mourn is to sympathise.

[1] G. M. Trevelyan, *The Life of John Bright*, pp. 42-3.

[2] *Op. cit.*, p. 65.

In so showing sympathy men display the spirit of Jesus and enter the fellowship of His sufferings, who 'Himself took our infirmities and bore our sicknesses' (Matt. 8.16-17). It is to share in the blessedness of God in His redeeming purpose. (See I Tim. 1.11. The word here translated 'blessed' is the same as is used in the Beatitudes.) 'Happiness', it has been said, 'is a great love and much serving.'

There are many kinds of anodyne and dope offered to men in the modern world: drink, gambling, the cinema in some of its productions. Religion, even what has been thought to be the Christian religion, has at times been used as dope; as both Karl Marx and Charles Kingsley, independently though almost simultaneously, recognised. It is all too easy to stifle the imagination and like Dives to pass Lazarus in the street every day without feeling that he is any concern of ours. Many men and women put on the whole armour of selfishness against the needs of others. But a true Christianity is a foe to insensitiveness and callousness. 'Christ taught us to care', wrote von Hügel. 'Caring is the great thing. Caring matters most.' Christianity quickens the imagination and awakens the sympathy.

The secret of life, its true blessing, is hidden from hardness and indifference. The higher the life the more sensitive it is. That is true physically. It is no less true spiritually. 'If ever we stop being dissatisfied it can only be because we have become insensitive' (A. D. Lindsay). 'To be perfect as our Father in heaven is perfect is no cloistered withdrawing from the contamination of an evil world, but to be like Him in kindness to the unthankful and evil, and through our own heart of compassion to see Him as a love which, without partiality, is concerned about the good of all His children and not least the sinful and wayward.'[1]

Such Christian 'mourning' has through the centuries been a power for righteousness. It leads men to the succour of the distressed and the reform of their conditions. Marius the Epicurean, in Pater's story, was thinking about the brutal-

[1] Oman, *Grace and Personality*, p. 100.

ities of the gladiatorial shows. 'What was needed,' he mused, 'was the heart that would make it impossible to witness all this, and the future would be with the forces which could beget this heart.'[1] The teaching of Jesus has created in generation after generation the heart that is sensitive to cruelty and wrong and often becomes God's instrument for its abolition. Such 'mourning' is costly, but it is creative and redemptive. 'The pleasures of each generation evaporate in the air. It is their pains that increase the spiritual momentum of the world' (Illingworth).

> For a tear is an intellectual thing
> And a sigh is the sword of an angel king
> And the bitter groan of a martyr's woe
> Is an arrow from the Almighty's bow.
>
> (BLAKE).

'Blessed are they that mourn: for they shall be comforted.' 'Comfort' nowadays suggests a snug arm-chair before the fire. But it comes from the same root as 'fortified', and it used to have a robuster meaning. That suggestion is also in the Greek. There is certainly the note of sympathy and gentle concern, but we shall not be far wrong if we translate it 'They shall be made strong'.

Some people's strength is all drawn from themselves. They are like isolated pools with limited reserves. Others are more like rivers. They do not produce or contain the power: it flows through them. The more they give, the more they are able to draw in. Their strength is not their own. It is given to them. The strength that God gives is available for those who care for others. For they are showing the spirit of Jesus. The power of God's Spirit fortifies them. They are 'strong in the strength which God supplies through His eternal Son'.

---

[1] *Marius the Epicurean*, II, p. 242.

IV

Blessed are the meek: for they shall inherit the earth.
Matt. 5.5.

MARK TWAIN said that this Beatitude clearly referred to
the British! 'Sir', said an Indian student, more seriously, to
a friend of mine, 'The Englishman may inherit the earth,
but if you called him meek he would be insulted.'

Meekness is not a popular virtue anywhere in the Western
world: perhaps anywhere at all in these modern days. This
is partly because it has many counterfeits, which are anything but lovely. To bear wrong uncomplainingly may not
be a Christian virtue at all; it may be cowardice or moral
indifference. Meekness is not the same thing as lying down
before injustice because we have not the courage or the
spirit to do anything else.

But meekness is also thought of little worth among us
because meekness itself, the real thing, is not valued or
admired. Pride, self-assertion, anger, pushfulness, are given
fine names and thought manly. *Nemo me impune lacessit:* no
one provokes *me* with impunity. That is the Roman and the
modern idea of a strong man. If you want to get on, you
must push and assert yourself. If you don't look after
number one, no one else will.

Meekness certainly is not tame resignation or lying down
under circumstances. Weakness is yielding to our nature:
meekness is mastery over it. The meek man is one who has
got himself out of the centre of the picture. 'His cosmos is
all ego', said Disraeli of an acquaintance; the truly meek
man 'denies himself'. He does not measure events by their
effect upon his own welfare or comfort. His main concern
is not for his own interests or reputation. He is ruled by love
for God and his neighbour. He seeks first the Kingdom of
God.

Jesus called Himself 'meek and lowly' (Matt. 11.29:
'gentle and humble' is Moffatt's rendering. See also Matt.

21.5.) and Paul speaks of the 'meekness and gentleness of Christ' (II Cor. 10.1.) That should make us think, and throw light upon meekness. For, as Watcyn Williams wrote, 'Nouns qualify adjectives as well as adjectives nouns. When the noun is Jesus, the adjective, whatever it be, is apt to lose some of its original meaning. It begins to acquire new shades of significance'.[1] Or in the words of John Oman,[2] 'If meekness is mere pliancy, as of the willow before the storm, He who offered us peace because He was meek and lowly in heart, must have been far astray about Himself'.

Think, for instance, of the anger of Jesus. Inhumanity or the misrepresentation of God, especially by religious teachers, roused Him to wrath. When the Pharisees and scribes objected to His healing the man with the withered hand on the Sabbath, 'He looked round about on them with anger, being grieved for the hardness of their hearts', their callous inhumanity; and also perhaps because they imputed their inhumanity to God, by claiming that they were acting in defence of His law, making as He said at another time, the word of God of none effect through their traditions (Mark 3.5, 7.13).

He was 'moved with indignation' when the disciples tried to prevent the children from coming to Him (Mark 10.13ff., R.V.). His anger drove Him to cleanse the Temple of those whose covetousness profaned the house of prayer and interfered with the worship of the Gentiles (Mark 11.15ff.). How stern were His words of condemnation for those who made children, and simple and innocent people generally, to stumble (Matt. 18.6f.); and for Peter when he tried to tempt Him away from the path to the Cross (Matt. 16.21-23).

If we learn of Christ, meekness must be consistent with abounding vitality, energetic pursuit of a purpose, and a detestation of hypocrisy and sham and inhumanity. Meekness is the opposite of self assertion or vindictiveness. The meek man does not make selfish demands on life. His

[1] *The Beatitudes in the Modern World*, p. 53.

[2] *Grace and Personality*, p. 95.

purpose will not be his own advancement or profit. But he may be a man of strong words and deeds and inflexible determination.

Abraham Lincoln gave a good illustration of meekness in a Presidential election address. 'I know there is a God and that He hates injustice and slavery. I see the storm coming and I know His hand is in it. If He has a place and work for me, and I believe He has, I am ready. I am nothing, but truth is everything.'[1] Lincoln could be terrible, but not in self-defence. Florence Nightingale could fight like a tigress for her wounded. Wilberforce pulled no punches in dealing with those who defended slavery. Elizabeth Fry was a gentler creature than Florence Nightingale and con-temporaries said that her 'courtly politeness' never failed; but neither did her determined persistence and insistence where the welfare of her prisoners was concerned. All four were meek in the Christian sense. They had forgotten themselves.

I was present not long ago at a presentation to a friend of mine who had celebrated his jubilee in the ministry. 'I have often seen you angry', said the chairman as he made the presentation, 'but never at anything that had been said or done to yourself. It was only when you thought someone else had been unjustly treated.' Absence of anger may mean absence of love.

Meekness cannot be identified with 'non-resistance'. But the meek man will choose the right weapon. Self control and positive goodwill may inspire a resistance that is clearly not apathy or cowardice and yet is equally clearly not mere retaliation. We may so present what W. E. Hocking calls 'a new idea' to the wrongdoer.[2] We cannot lay down in advance what Christian love may demand of us in the presence of an aggressor; love for the aggressor certainly, but also love for his victim and for the maintenance of justice and freedom. We may be called to silence or to

[1] Quoted by James Reid, *op. cit.*, p. 92.
[2] *Human Nature and its Remaking*, p. 352.

protest, to patient endurance or to the use of force, in order
to convey the message or make it possible for the aggressor
to hear it. 'Whatever the instrument employed, Jesus says
distinctly that blind pugnacity—retaliation—which simply
employs the weapon of the enemy on the instinct of the
moment, is a sin against man and God. . . . Something has to
be done, some choice of weapon made that will cost in
thought and self-control. The other cheek must be turned.
. . . The injured man . . . must go on bearing the pains and
cost of his choice of weapon, in the faith that in the end
victory, not for himself but for God, will be secured. It is
success for the Kingdom not for any individual moral effort
that Jesus promises.'[1]

The worldly despise the meek who will not push and fight
for position. Yet they are often afraid of them. There is
something there they cannot touch with their threats. When
Jesus stood before Pilate, armed in His meekness, it was
Pilate who was distressed; afraid of Caesar, afraid of losing
his job, afraid even of his mysterious prisoner. Meekness is
not weakness. Few of us have the right to speak from our
own experience but we have seen it true in others, that the
man who is really self-forgetful and devoted to the service
of God and His Kingdom has the secret of heroism and
strength.

'Now I know', says a character in a modern novel, 'that
strength is something more than the trampling of others into
the dust that we ourselves may have a clear road. It is something harder and much less triumphant than that. It is the
standing aside to let somebody else pass on.'[2] Someone has
said that a man may do a great deal of good if he does not
care who gets the credit. It is the strength of meekness to be
ready to see the cause for which he strives prosper in the
hands of another and another reap where he has sown.
T. H. Huxley wrote a New Year resolution in his diary on
January 1st, 1857. 'To smite all humbugs, however big; to

[1] R. H. Strachan, *The Authority of Christian Experience*, p. 206.

[2] Thurston, *John Chilcote, M.P.*, p. 309.

give a nobler tone to science; to set an example of abstinence from petty personal controversies and of toleration for everything but lying; to be indifferent as to whether the work is recognised as mine or not, so long as it is done.'

Yet how shall the meek 'inherit the earth'? Heaven perhaps, but scarcely the earth! Meekness may be worthy of all admiration but in outward possession the world belongs to the strong and grasping. It must be admitted frankly that it is not easy to understand precisely what our Lord meant.

The Beatitude is an Old Testament echo. 'The meek shall inherit the earth' (Ps. 37.11; cf. also Num. 12.3). The phrase 'inherit the earth' or 'inherit the land' is frequently used in the Old Testament in the literal sense about the possession of the Promised Land. Later the phrase was used figuratively, as in the 37th Psalm, of entering into possession of Divine blessing. In the New Testament the Christian inheritance is spoken of as 'eternal life', 'salvation', 'the promises', and in other ways, but the characteristic and most frequent description of the inheritance is the Kingdom of God, as reference to a concordance will show. It is possible that Jesus, using the phrase in its figurative Old Testament sense, means that the Kingdom of God is the Promised Land of the New Covenant, and is 'the earth' of this Beatitude.

Or did He mean that they alone really possess the world who use it aright, as its Creator meant it to be used, that they make the most of life who see the earth and themselves as parts and instruments of the Divine purpose? Material ownership does not necessarily bring true possession. The rich man who buys a great painting to hang on his walls may not 'possess' it as truly as the poor man who pays his half crown to see round the castle. The man who is receptive and objective, and not possessive or assertive in his attitude to life, gets the most out of it.

Izaak Walton has the idea. 'I could there sit quietly, and looking on the waters see fishes leaping at flies of several shapes and colours. Looking on the hills, I could behold them spotted with woods and groves. Looking down the meadows, I could see a boy gathering lilies and ladysmocks, and there a girle cropping columbines and cowslips, all to make garlands suitable to this present month of May. As I thus sate, joying in mine own happy condition, I did thankfully remember what my Saviour said, that the meek possess the earth.'

Cowper has much the same thought in 'The Winter Morning Walk' (Book V of *The Task*):

> He looks abroad into the varied fields
> Of Nature, and though poor perhaps, compared
> With those whose mansions glitter in his sight,
> Calls the delightful scenery all his own,
> > His to enjoy
> With a propriety that none can feel
> But who with filial confidence inspired
> Can lift to heaven an unpresumptuous eye
> And smiling say—'My Father made them all'.

Most of us disinherit ourselves from the full enjoyment of the estate to which God has made us heirs. There is much that we own or might own that we do not truly possess. A man may own a Bible but it is not really his if it only lies on a table in the parlour, as a piece of furniture, as it so often used to and in some houses still does, or accumulates dust in a bookshelf. It only becomes his own if he uses it, turns it into food for his spiritual life. There are treasures in divine grace, in forgiveness and redemption and sanctification, which we might inherit but to which we do not lay claim. The meek would inherit them.

Or is Jesus saying again here what He said at another time, that food and clothing and social prosperity were not to be got by struggle and grab? Seek first the Kingdom of God, and His righteousness, He said, and all these things shall be added unto you (Matt. 6.24-34). Do any of us really inherit the earth in this generation? Wars and preparations for war impoverish the world. Natural resources are ill applied or destroyed. Many people go under-nourished. The nations keep suspicious watch on one another and spend their money for that which is not bread and their labour for that which satisfieth not. We cannot ignore the facts, though it does not follow that the blame for them is to be evenly distributed.

As has been said above, it is not to be assumed that, for example, unilateral disarmament is the Christian way in such a world situation. It is not easy to see the policy for a Christian statesman in such a situation as ours, or how far one country can go alone. But if the Western powers and China and the Soviet bloc together would follow the way of Christ, then the earth would yield her increase (Ps. 67).

Seek the Kingdom of God, said Jesus. Join in fellowship in mutual service and you can have all you need. The earth with all its treasures is yours to inherit. But the team spirit, not the spirit of the rich fool is needed. He said *my* goods, because he was a fool. Jesus would have us say '*our* daily bread'. Then there would be enough for all. Of course it sounds fantastic, but is it not true? If the nations followed the way of meekness, lived in the spirit of Christ, food, clothing, peace and plenty *would* be added to us. But covetousness and aggression, which are the antithesis of meekness, mean the denial of brotherhood, extremes of wealth and poverty, economic disaster and war. Meekness—the co-operative and not the egotistic mind—is sound politics and economics as well as sound religion. Until we learn to be meek mankind will never inherit the earth. The victories of violence are ephemeral and sow the seeds of their own destruction. The victories of meekness endure.

And perhaps for some readers it may be well to add, do not too hastily dismiss the previous paragraphs as an unworthy materialising of spiritual truth. The Bible itself is against us if we seek to separate soul and body, heaven and earth, spiritual and material. What God has joined together let no man separate.

V

Blessed are they which do hunger and thirst after right-
eousness: for they shall be filled. Matt. 5.6.
Blessed are ye that hunger now: for ye shall be filled.
Luke 6.21.

FEW of us know from personal experience the ravenous
longing of a starving man or the agony of a parched throat,
but we know enough to realise that hunger and thirst are
the master appetites of human nature. Till they are satisfied
a man has little thought to spare for other things. Indeed,
after a point he *cannot* care for other things: no man, it has
been said, can be a hero, a lover or a poet, unless he has
recently had something to eat. These are strong words that
Jesus uses.

Here again, as in the Beatitude about poverty, Luke
apparently stresses a physical condition in contrast to
Matthew's spiritual emphasis. Once again Luke's report
may give the startling, challenging, original words, but
Matthew's paraphrase, if it is one, gives the sense: Luke
records the aphorism, Matthew adds the interpretation.

The metaphor is often used in the Bible. The writer of
Psalm 107 uses both the literal and the metaphorical sense
within a few verses. He reminds us of the children of Israel
in the Exodus, fainting for hunger and thirst, and of God's
deliverance (vv. 4, 5.) So God satisfies the longing soul and
fills the hungry soul with goodness (v. 9.) (cf. Job 23.12;
Isa. 49.10, 55.1-2; Ps. 42.1-2; Amos 8.11f.; Rev. 22.17).
The image of a feast is employed more than once by Jesus
for the satisfactions of the Kingdom of God (e.g. Matt.
8.11, 22.1-10; Luke 22.30; cf. also John 6.26-59).

This Beatitude challenges us. Do we care for righteousness
with anything like the intensity with which the hungry
man craves food? Blessed, says Jesus, are the men and
women who long for goodness more than for anything else.
Are we restless and unhappy unless we are making progress

in the growth of a Christ-like character, unless we see justice triumphing in the life of the world? Have we that sort of enthusiasm for God and His service? How few of us could say, yes. My meat is to do the will of God, said Jesus (John 4.34). Goodness would be, as we say, 'meat and drink' to one who truly followed Him.

This metaphor of hunger and thirst is much too strong for most of our religion. Our concern for goodness is apt to be half-hearted and occasional. We rather distrust strenuous enthusiasm.

> For I am tolerant, generous, keep no rules
>   And the age honours me.
> Thank God, I am not as these rigid fools,
>   Even as this Pharisee.[1]

Many Christians are put to shame by the self-sacrificing toil of many a communist, spurred on by his fierce dissatisfaction over the state of the world. We may not like his programme or his methods but he does forget himself in his cause as too few of us Christians do.[2] Jesus loved the enthusiast who gave himself without reserve. He liked energetic action, as in the men who broke a way through the roof for their paralysed friend (Luke 5.18-26). He praised the man who banged on the door till he got an answer (Luke 11.5-8). He wanted men to show that kind of determination in the affairs of religion (Luke 11.9-13). 'When the soul shares the purpose of God, not coldly but with eager desire', writes J. H. Oldham, 'then there is a new fact in the spiritual world. A new way is opened whereby the Lord can enter into the hearts of men.'

'Righteousness' is a rich word, and steeped in Old Testament associations. Moffatt translates it here as 'goodness'

[1] Alice Meynell, *The Newer Vain Glory*.

[2] Everyone should read *The God that Failed*, edited by Crossman (Harper & Brothers). It is an illuminating revelation of both the strength and the weakness of communism in the experience of six men who were once communists themselves.

and that has the advantage of making it more real to modern ears. The word in the prophets could often be translated by 'justice', though the thought of compassion and mercy must be associated with it. It is not a merely ethical term. On the human side it involves a right relation to God, evidenced in a life of justice and generosity to one's fellows. On the divine side it is God's fulfilment of His own purposes of justice and mercy. It includes both corporate and personal obedience. It is a way of life that springs from right relations with God. 'What doth the Lord require of thee but to do justly and to love mercy and to walk humbly with thy God' (Micah 6.8). You cannot put Christian righteousness into a Decalogue or into ten times ten regulations. That may be the Judaism of the scribes; it is not Christianity. All the law is summed up in the twofold commandment of love to God and love to man.

Man is hungry and thirsty by nature but he is not always wise enough to seek good food. A hungry child may eat the tempting but poisonous berries from the hedge. The best of us are like children slowly learning to tell good food from bad. We snatch at anything that promises satisfaction. That is the root of adventure and of tragedy.

We may lose our spiritual appetites for a time by seeking satisfaction on low levels, as a child may spoil his appetite for dinner by too many sweets. We spend our money for that which is not bread and our labour for that which satisfieth not (Isa. 55.2). So Jesus cries, 'Alas for you who are full'. Their spiritual appetite is gone. Those whose hunger is for wealth or pleasure are never satisfied. Appetite cries Give! Give! (Prov. 30.15). Satiated, 'fed up', do not mean the same as 'satisfied'.

But those who hunger for righteousness, they shall be satisfied, says Jesus. This hunger is not the gnawing of starvation, or the fruitless hunger of the prodigal in the far country. It is the healthful appetite of children at their father's table. The supply is proportioned to the hunger. 'There is as much in our Lord's pantry', writes Samuel

Rutherfurd in his quaint way, 'as will satisfy all His bairns:
and as much wine in His cellar as will quench all their thirst.
Hunger on: for there is meat in hunger for Christ: go never
from Him but fash[1] Him (who yet is pleased with the
importunity of hungry souls) with a dishful of hungry desires
till He fill you.'

Desire for righteousness is already righteousness. To
desire goodness is in a measure to be already good. This
is a blessing upon unfulfilled aspiration. He who seeks to
respond to the demand of love on him, finds a relation to
God and others which is its own satisfaction. It is love that
makes him hunger. It is fellowship with God that makes
him thirst. And yet he is always being satisfied. Bernard of
Clairvaux expresses it in one of the loveliest of all hymns:

> From the best bliss that earth imparts
> We turn unfilled to Thee again.
>
> We taste Thee, O Thou living Bread,
>   And long to feast upon Thee still.
> We drink of Thee, the Fountain Head,
>   And thirst our souls from Thee to fill.

Before God can feed the soul there must be hunger. It is
true even of nourishment for the body that you cannot feed
a child who will not eat. With the food of the mind and the
spirit you are as powerless to give it to a child till he is
hungry for it, as God is to give it to you. Nothing so
gladdens a true father and mother as to find in their child
the stirring of a thirst for knowledge, of a love of beauty,
of a desire for goodness. We can do something to stimulate
the appetite, but it must be there before we can satisfy it.
The man who is already satisfied will never learn. 'He hath
filled the hungry with good things' (Luke 1.53)—that is
true in music, in science, and in religion. It is the hungry who
are filled.

So in the realm of social righteousness is it not true that

[1] Bother.

we do not care enough? How often do we meet a divine discontent with things as they are in society and in international relations along with a hunger for the time when justice will prevail. Of course there is plenty of discontent of a kind, an annoyance with our own discomfort and austerity and insecurity. But is there much real positive longing for international fellowship and justice? Men cannot have what they do not hunger for.

'It is your Father's good pleasure to give you the Kingdom.' One of Christ's great gifts is the gift of hope—which is not the same thing as what is usually called optimism. He gives the assurance of the ultimate triumph of the divine will, the establishment of His Kingdom of righteousness, joy, and peace. And it comes first in the hearts of those who hunger for it.

VI

> Blessed are the merciful for they shall obtain mercy.
> Matt. 5.7.

ONE of the temptations of a sensitive conscience is censoriousness. If we 'hunger and thirst after righteousness' we are apt to confuse harshness with a conscientious stand for the right. Some ardent seekers after the good life are very difficult to live with. They are sure that their own list of do's and don't's must be obligatory for everybody. In matters where the New Testament leaves Christians free to make their own decision, they try to bind men's consciences in a new legalism. It does not seem to occur to them that Christians may legitimateiy differ about methods, and that it is dangerous to exalt one's own judgments to the status of an eleventh commandment. The Apostle Paul was wiser. There is something wrong with our following of Jesus if it makes us hard and denunciatory. The spirit and methods of some of our campaigns are open to question. Conscience might lead us to be sympathetic and understanding—lest we also be tempted, and remembering our own failures. But it can make us censorious and condemnatory. The Christian, says Jesus, must temper his eager search for righteousness with a spirit of gentleness and mercy.

Mercy in the biblical sense is something much wider than letting the offender off his deserved punishment, as in 'the king's prerogative of mercy'. It means compassion, 'suffering with'; sympathy, 'feeling with'; pity and forgiveness. It means the power to see life from the other's point of view. Love is perhaps the nearest equivalent to the Hebrew *Hesed* which is one of the great words of the Old Testament, occurring about one hundred and fifty times. It is used mostly of God's attitude to men, but sometimes of the spirit men ought to show to one another.[1]

[1] See a useful discussion by T. H. Robinson, *Moffatt Commentary on St. Matthew*, p. 30.

Love, or mercy, in the biblical sense is not only a matter of the emotions; it means active goodwill. But it does include the feelings. We say sometimes, rather too easily, that we cannot control our feelings. But mercy begins in the thoughts, in cultivating a kindly judgment, not of the fault, but of the wrong-doer. Feeling can be educated by control instead of by free indulgence, and by the steady mastery of the imagination. People 'nurse their grievances', as we say: they brood over real or imagined injustices. They keep up feuds for years. They watch for a chance to 'pay back' the other man. Such brooding can hatch a mere spark of dislike into a blaze of hatred. But mercy too can be nurtured in our thoughts and feelings by kindly care. Feeling and action act and react upon one another. Feelings frequently indulged in word or deed get stronger, whether for good or evil. And the effort to render practical help to one we dislike will nourish liking.

For, of course, mercy can never stop at feelings, though it includes them. G. M. Trevelyan in his *Life of John Bright* tells a story of Jacob Bright, John's father. One day he was coming up the hill from town to his home, and found a poor neighbour in great trouble on the road. His horse had met with an accident and had had to be killed. People were crowding round the man saying how sorry they were. To one who kept on repeating this most loudly, Jacob Bright said: 'I am sorry five pounds. How much are you sorry?' And Jacob Bright passed round the hat to buy the man another horse.

That is in the spirit of Jesus. Mercy is not emotion, but emotion that leads to action. Aristotle seems to have regarded pity as a troublesome emotion to be purged harmlessly out of the system in beholding tragic drama.[1] Whether that is a misunderstanding of Aristotle's famous words or not, in the New Testament pity which does nothing is a hateful hypocrisy (e.g. I John 3.16-18; Jas. 2.13ff.). To Jesus, mercy was to be harnessed to kindly and redemptive

[1] See, for example, *Tragedy* by W. McNeile Dixon, pp. 112ff.

action. 'Inasmuch as ye *did* it', He said. And the scribe
had grasped the point of the story of the Good Samaritan
when he identified the 'neighbour' as the one who *showed
mercy* by giving practical help (Luke 10.37). And how often
in the Gospels we read that Jesus 'had compassion'. The
particular Greek adjective used in this Beatitude is found
in the New Testament again only in Heb. 2.17, describing
Jesus as 'a merciful and faithful high priest', but the
corresponding verb 'to obtain mercy' or 'to show mercy' is
frequent in the New Testament. And there are several other
words in the Bible for mercy and merciful. Indeed the
thought is everywhere. It is one of the central Biblical
themes.

The Bible is full of the mercy of God. His servants the
prophets preach it. Amos in the name of the Lord fiercely
denounces the cruelties of aggressive war and the oppression
of the helpless poor. Hosea's book is radiant with tender-
ness for the unworthy woman who had wrecked his life.
The Second Isaiah has a great vision of one to come who
would suffer for men and with men as the servant of God.
The Old Testament reveals a progress in pity.

Most of all, we see the mercy of God incarnate in Jesus
Himself. How revealing is that incident of the woman
caught in adultery and thrust into His presence to be
castigated—as her accusers hoped—by the wrath of this
religious teacher before she was dragged off to punishment.
But the indignation of Jesus was rather for those pitiless
faces than for their cowering victim. 'Let him that is without
sin among you cast the first stone', He said. And they
slunk off one by one. 'Neither do I condemn thee. Go and
sin no more.' Mercy like that is redemptive. If there was
anything in that wretched woman's heart to appeal to, the
cruel pitilessness of these men would have crushed it out.
And Jesus' way is God's way. 'For mercy, pity, peace and
love is God our Father dear', sings Blake. What light that
casts on life and its dark places.

No man can have friends or move among his fellows with

a sympathetic heart without continually finding tragedy and suffering, if indeed he does not meet them on his own door step. What has God to say? The one hundred and third Psalm is one way of putting the Bible answer. 'Like as a father pitieth his children, so the Lord pitieth them that fear him.'[1] You care when your child is in trouble. So does God for you. You cannot always take your child out of his trouble: sometimes you know it would not be good for him if you did. But you can help him *in* his trouble. You stand by him in sympathy. You give him courage and strength. So does God for you in your troubles. And if it is your sin that has found you out and you bow in your penitence before God as that woman did at the feet of Jesus, you will hear the voice of God's mercy saying: 'Neither do I condemn thee. Go and sin no more.'

This truth of the mercy of God has consequences for our own living. Real religion means becoming like your God—getting His spirit into your own lives. Worship implies that: we 'become inly liker that we kneel before'. 'Beloved, if God so loved us we ought to love one another.' The story of the unforgiving debtor challenges us once again (Matt. 18.23ff.). 'The hand on his brother's throat destroys the servant's own forgiveness. He cannot be at once a rapacious creditor and a discharged bankrupt.' I had mercy on you, said his lord. Why had you no mercy on your fellow? I rescind my forgiveness of your debt. 'So likewise shall my heavenly Father do also unto you, if ye from your hearts forgive not every one his brother their trespasses.'

Wherever there is mercy in human life it is in response to God's call. Jerome K. Jerome speaks somewhere of primitive man in his savagery and brutality: 'pitiless, deaf, blind, groping in the darkness, not knowing even himself. Then came the dim first standard bearer of the Lord, the man who first felt pity. Savage, brutish, dumb, staring down at some hurt creature, his dull eyes troubled by a strange new pain he understood not. And suddenly as he stooped there must

[1] I.e. those who reverence Him, not those who are frightened of Him.

have come a great light into his eyes. Man had heard God's voice across the deep and had made answer.' God's voice calls us to pity.

But what a commentary that is on the world situation. Thank God, we can find on all hands works of mercy, perhaps more widespread and efficient than ever before. But this generation has witnessed no less a widespread increase in sheer pitiless brutality in men's dealings with each other. There has always been brutality in the world, but we have seen it stalk the earth unashamedly, clothed in fine theories about living space and superior races and the goal of a classless society. And the instruments on which brutality can lay its hands get more terribly efficient day by day. Power accumulates but mercy withers.

I cannot believe it is the will of God that we should stand by and watch brutality batter the weak and destroy the liberty of small nations. The very pity of God can be stern against the pitiless, as witness the Bible. Love in defence of the weak can speak hard words and do grim deeds. War is unspeakably horrible, but unrestrained pitiless aggression and the crushing of human freedom are more horrible still. Yet the fact that Christian men trying to be true to their Lord, hating violence and loving peace, have felt driven to such a conclusion only demonstrates the more poignantly how mercy has been driven from the world.[1]

We must think of this also in personal terms. Unless mercy is expressed in our own lives we have no right to abuse dictators and totalitarian régimes. So far as we ourselves have power we must be pitiful in our use of it. There are little men who are bullies: Hitlers in the home or the workshop. There are women who are merciless in their treatment of shop assistants and waitresses, though their victims are happily not so defenceless as they once were.

Of all the many calls for mercy at this hour surely none is more inescapable and heart moving than that of the

[1] I gave my reasons for rejecting the pacifist position at some length in *The Christian as Soldier*, now out of print.

refugees. Millions of people throughout Europe and the Middle East (to say nothing of Korea) are existing in squalor and misery, in spite of the efforts made to help them. As I write, those who know report a continuing problem of heart-rending magnitude. There are at least nine million refugees in Western Germany, 300,000 in Austria, 700,000 in Greece, 750,000 in Palestine. Millions live in grim camps. Thousands exist in cellars, crude shelters, and caves. They need the physical necessities of life, food, medical supplies, clothing, housing. But even worse than physical need is the bewilderment and despair, the numbing sense of being unwanted, the absence of any future to live for. They need practical schemes of hope and rehabilitation, education, occupation, succour for the helpless aged, and unremitting effort to restore them to responsible citizenship. The Inter-Church Aid and Refugee Service Department of the British Council of Churches (5 Southampton Place, London, W.C.1) can use our gifts in works of Christ-like mercy.

Take one other illustration. Society now growingly recognises the place of redemptive as well as punitive action in the treatment of the criminal. Contact with criminals not seldom reveals that the causes for their fall might well have upset ourselves, and also the fine qualities that survive in them. There is a place for punishment. There is need to protect society. But there is need for mercy, too, for the effort to re-establish them as useful citizens. Such humanitarian work has many disappointments. Some reject the help that is offered. Others exploit and betray those who are kind to them. But the vindictive treatment of the past did not mean a world with less crime, and the Christian can never forget the man in the criminal. Jesus said His job was looking for lost people, and His primary concern to get men back where they ought to be, home, their earthly home, and the fellowship of their heavenly Father too (Luke 15).

There is a converse to all this. If it is the voice of God

that calls to mercy, the man who stifles the voice of God will lack mercy. Behind the pitilessness of the modern world is the godlessness of the modern world. That is cause and effect. The growth of naked and unashamed brutality has gone with an avowed return to paganism. The Bible tells of a growing understanding of pity, because it is the story of the encounter of the Spirit of God with the spirits of men. The brute lurks in each of us, despite our civilisation and culture. The beast will emerge out of the dark recesses of our selfish hearts if it is not chained and tamed. And 'civilisation' does not tame the beast in man. Let history and the newspaper bear record of that. Nothing can surely feed the springs of mercy in human life but a continually renewed fellowship with the God of mercy who can cleanse the pitilessness out of our hearts and teach us how to love our fellows as He has first loved us (Matt. 18.21-35; Luke 17.3-4; Mark 11.25-26).

'They shall obtain mercy.' From men? Sometimes. But it was not so with Jesus Himself. You cannot be sure that if you care for the needs of others someone will care for you. 'Give and it shall be given you' is often true, but there are many exceptions if it be taken literally. Certainly mercy blesses him that gives as well as him that takes. No man ever showed mercy without receiving a blessing in his own heart. Portia's speech in *The Merchant of Venice* is a valuable commentary on this Beatitude and not least in the suggestion that we should be merciful to man because we need and hope for mercy from God.

Ecclesiasticus makes the same point:

He that taketh vengeance shall find vengeance from the
    Lord,
And will surely make firm his sins.
Forgive thy neighbour the hurt that he hath done thee;
And then thy sins shall be pardoned when thou prayest.

Man cherisheth anger against man;
And doth he seek healing from the Lord?
Upon a man like himself he hath no mercy
And doth he make supplication for his own sins?

Is that then what Jesus meant? He cannot have meant that we can earn mercy or establish a claim upon God. Mercy is precisely that which one does not earn or deserve, to which one has no right. Yet Jesus does say many times that we must be ready to forgive if we are to receive God's forgiveness. He taught that unless forgiveness flows out of a man's heart, there is no room in it for the forgiveness of God. This is no arbitrary bargain: if you forgive him, I will forgive you. It is a question of the very nature of forgiveness, which is not a legal act but a spiritual one. Its essence is restoration to fellowship. Fellowship with a merciful God is impossible except to the merciful.[1]

'Let all bitterness and wrath and anger and clamour and evil speaking be put away from you, with all malice: and be ye kind one to another, tender hearted, forgiving one another, even as God for Christ's sake hath forgiven you (Eph. 4.31-32). 'Be ye therefore merciful, as your Father also is merciful' (Luke 6.36).

[1] For a fuller discussion of forgiveness see my book, *The Lord's Prayer*, Chapter VII.

VII

Blessed are the pure in heart: for they shall see God.
Matt. 5.8.

IN the Book of Esther (1.14) the seven princes of Media
and Persia who stood next in honour to Ahasuerus are
described as those that 'saw the king's face'. And Jesus once
said, using, I think, this same metaphor from an Oriental
court, that the angels who look after little children always
behold the face of the Father in heaven. They have immediate access to the divine presence, the right of audience.
They are among the most favoured in court. So it is the pure
in heart that are 'far ben' with God, to use the Scots expression, in His inmost fellowship (cf. Ps. 24.3-5).

After Pascal's death a servant discovered, sewn into his
coat, a scrap of parchment which apparently he had always
carried with him. It was a record in broken words of an
overwhelming ecstatic experience of the Divine Presence.
Among its breathless phrases is one which reads like a cry
of amazement: 'Not the God of philosophers and of
scholars.' *Non des philosophes et des savants!* The great
scientist and philosopher had discovered that God revealed
Himself not to the wise and prudent, but to babes, not to
learning but to love, to the pure in heart (cf. Matt. 11.25).

As with all the Beatitudes, the promise of this one has a
double fulfilment. Now and in the future the pure in heart
shall see God. Of the nature of the heavenly vision we do not
know and cannot speak: 'Eye hath not seen nor ear heard,
neither hath it entered into the heart of man to conceive'
(I Cor. 2.9). 'It doth not yet appear what we shall be'
(I John 3.2). But in measure there is a divine vision for this
world too. The pure in heart are aware of a reality that most
of us miss. They are sure of God.

Of course the reference to eyes and 'heart' is metaphorical.
The Jewish use of bodily organs as seats of intellectual,

emotional or moral life, even if originally literal, had become figurative. 'Heart' may be understood here in prosaic language to mean the interior life of the personality. When the heart is used metaphorically in modern English it means the emotions and affections, but the biblical use is wider. Wheeler Robinson says that in 851 uses of 'heart' in the Old Testament in one-third of the total number it means the personality as a whole. Some of the remaining two-thirds stress the emotions, but in many the intellect and the will are emphasised. The other uses of the expression in the teaching of Jesus throw light upon the Beatitude, e.g., 'Where your treasure is, there will your heart be also' (Matt. 6.21). 'Out of the abundance of the heart the mouth speaketh. A good man out of the good treasure of the heart bringeth forth good things: and an evil man out of the evil treasure bringeth forth evil things' (Matt. 12.34-35; cf. Matt. 15.19). The emphasis of Jesus here is, no doubt, on the inner reality of the soul, compared with external appearances (see Chapter I). It is a pure *heart* that is needed.

The vision of God is again a frequent metaphor for communion with God, consciousness of His presence, a relationship to Him of awe, love, and obedience, God dwelling in us and we in God. The image is a favourite one with the mystics. In a survey of the characteristics of mysticism, in his book *Christian Mysticism*, Dean Inge says that mysticism as a type of religion rests on four articles of faith. First, the soul, as well as the body, can see and perceive. We possess an organ for discerning spiritual truth which is as reliable in its proper sphere as the organs of sensation in theirs. Second, man in order to know God, must be a partaker of the Divine nature. A Divine spark already shines within us, to be searched for and tended. The third article is that only the pure in heart can see God. Sensuality and selfishness are absolute disqualifications. And, fourthly, the guide on the upward path is love.[1]

Purity of heart has come to be associated almost

[1] *Op. cit.*, pp. 6-8.

exclusively with sex. But that is not what Jesus has in mind here. The pure in heart are the sincere and single minded. Purity here means freedom from any admixture of base matter, as we speak of pure food, pure water, and so forth. A pure heart is one that is absolutely sincere and single-minded in its desire to love and serve God. The opposite of the pure in heart is the double-minded man who is unstable in all his ways (Jas. 1.8)—the half-hearted man.

To Jesus, the pure hearted, all life was a parable of God. Wherever He turned in the world of nature or of humanity what He saw spoke to Him of the Divine. Nature was a sacrament of the Divine Presence. The ways of birds and beasts, the sunset and the wind, the flowers, all had a word to speak. Wordsworth writes in *The Excursion* of the child who picks up a shell and putting it to his ear thinks he hears the murmuring of the sea—

> Even such a shell the universe itself
> Is to the ear of Faith: and there are times
> I doubt not, when to you it doth impart
> Authentic tidings of invisible things.

That is true to the thought of Jesus. We can well believe that the words attributed to Him in the Oxyrhynchus Papyri are indeed from His lips. 'Jesus saith: Ye ask who are those that draw us to the Kingdom if the Kingdom is in heaven? The fowls of the air and all the beasts that are under the earth or upon the earth, and the fishes of the sea, these are they which draw you, and the Kingdom of heaven is within you and whosoever shall know himself shall find it.'

The spiritual world and the natural are both products of the same Mind and Purpose. Nature without and human nature within illumine each other and both in spite of sin point to the God who made them. Human fatherhood points to the Father in heaven. 'If ye then, being evil, know how to give good gifts unto your children: how much more shall your heavenly Father give the Holy Spirit to them that ask him?' (Luke 11.13). This visible world, says

St. Paul, is designed to make known the invisible things of God (Rom. 1.20). So if we are pure in heart we shall see God in the beauty of nature and of human nature, and in the appeal of men's need.

Is not this too the key to purity in the popular sense of the word: to look at the other sex not with a lustful eye, as instruments of our pleasure, but as temples of the divine, and as personalities to be respected. 'The rake and the prude', it has been said, 'are both far from the Kingdom of God.' It is wrong to think of sex relations as an opportunity for selfish impersonal gratification, or on the other hand as inherently shameful. Many fail to achieve mastery in this realm because they do not seek goodness in the whole life but try to deal with this temptation in isolation.

A pure heart is one that is absolutely sincere in its desire to serve and love God. Single-hearted search is the condition of achievement in any realm. How greatly Jesus valued sincerity! It comes out again and again in the Gospels. Take, for example, the story of the man who came gushing to Him about his desire to follow. 'Lord, I will follow thee whithersoever thou goest.' 'Man', said Jesus in effect, 'Do you know what you are saying? Do you mean it? Following me is no picnic. Foxes have holes and birds of the air have nests; but the Son of man hath not where to lay his head (Luke 9.57-58). I don't want lip-service and fine words.'

Who of us can stand this test of utter sincerity? We half-believe. At times we are ready to do anything to prove our loyalty to Christ. But at other times we are slack and half-hearted. We have much need to pray—

> 'Look not on our misusings of Thy grace,
> Our prayer so languid and our faith so dim.'

And so we seldom 'see God', are seldom sure of His presence.

The vision of God is a spiritual vision and is dependent upon spiritual qualifications. Jesus was the image of the invisible God (Col. 1.15), yet to look even on Him with the eyes of flesh was not to see God. To many He was a heretic, a dangerous political rebel, an unrealistic dreamer, an unpatriotic traitor, a madman. To see God even in Jesus needs the pure heart,—today as well as then.

VIII

Blessed are the peacemakers: for they shall be called
the children of God (Matt. 5.9)

THERE is committed to Christians in St. Paul's great phrase
the ministry of reconciliation. It is their task to put an end
to quarrels, to mend broken fellowship, to make peace.

But though this sentence is in harmony with the teaching
of the Apostle, it is important to remember that when he
used the phrase (II Cor. 5.18) he was thinking of peace with
God, not peace among men. That is indeed the right place
to begin any discussion of peace making. All human
quarrels are at bottom symptoms of a broken peace with
God. The good news of the Christian message is that God,
righteously angry with man's flouting of the laws of justice
and love, has nevertheless taken the initiative in removing
everything that made for estrangement. In Christ, in His
life and teaching, and in His death when love and sin met in
ultimate conflict, God was reconciling the world to Himself, not reckoning their trespasses against them. God has
made peace, and Christians like ambassadors are sent to
beg men to accept peace at God's hands and on His terms.

No man can be an effective peace maker who is not himself at peace in his inner life, until the war in his own nature
is at an end, and the turmoil of conflicting desires and
ambitions has found unity in obedience. H. G. Wells, in
The History of Mr. Polly, said of one of his characters:
'He was not so much a human being as a civil war.' And
there can be no fundamental and lasting peace among men
until there is a common allegiance to an authority that
is above all our sectional sovereignties and a purpose that
takes up into itself our rival plans. In His will is our peace,
said Dante. The causes of war and of all quarrels are to be
found in the spirits of men and women, in selfishness, greed,
fear, and pride.

In the last talk of Jesus with His disciples as the Fourth Gospel records it, He declares that His legacy to them is peace. That is a hard saying. Now as then anxiety, care, and fear dominate men's hearts. Peace of mind seems unattainable to a thinking man. Indeed, is it not positively right that we should be concerned and anxious in days like these? Jesus at another time said that He came to bring not peace, but a sword. That seems more realistic. How is it that St. Paul includes peace among the fruit of the Spirit? What did our Lord mean by saying it was one of the gifts He gave to His disciples?

Some kinds of peace are in fact un-Christian. There is a peace of indifference. Some people 'couldn't care less' if there are millions of homeless refugees and displaced persons, if the weary and desolate Koreans plod back and forth in the track of war till they can plod no longer. Some people take for granted the need of the sick and lonely around them, as Dives accepted Lazarus as part of the street scenery. If he ever noticed Lazarus he ignored him; he just couldn't be bothered. Jesus denounced this self-contained life with indignation. His was the peace of a soul that was dead; the peace of a stagnant pond with a green scum of selfishness on top.

Even some Christians have been so false to their Lord as to use religion to counsel resignation and acceptance of the world as it is. They have told men to accept disease and disaster as 'the will of God'. It is not so long ago since some of them sang in their churches

> The rich man in his castle,
> The poor man at his gate,
> God made them, high or lowly,
> And order'd their estate.

To such ways of thinking Jesus would certainly say, I came to bring not peace but a sword. True religion is no opiate. It will not allow men to be contented with a world that is unjust and out of joint. It will not lead men to say, 'It's all right', when it isn't.

Peacemaking, like all the virtues, has its counterfeits. It is not the same thing as cowardice or love of a quiet life. One can often avoid a dispute by leaving it to others to stand up for the right. One can let the other fellow have it all his own way because he is bigger than you are or shouts louder. It may be human and prudent to do that, but it is hardly Christian peace making. 'When Martin Luther having nailed his theses to the church door at Wittenberg, walked into the imperial council hall of Charles V to face the charge of heresy, an old knight touched him on the shoulder with his gauntlet, saying: "Little monk, you are taking a step I like and which neither I nor many a commander in our fiercest battles, would take." '[1]

The peace-at-any-price people, saying peace, peace, where there is no peace, may be the foes of real peacemaking. The true peacemaker has often to be a fighter, though not always or only with weapons. Pugnacity is not necessarily bad or un-Christian. It is good to be aggressive in some circumstances. Christianity sublimates pugnacity, it does not destroy it. Paul could claim to have fought a good fight (II Tim. 4.7) and could exhort Timothy to 'fight the good fight of faith' (I Tim. 6.12). To say this is not of course to suggest that it provides a Christian justification for war: that is quite a different issue. Many honest pacifists are most healthily pugnacious in good causes and without any inconsistency.

Peacemaking is not to be confused with patching things up. There are times when bits of wire or even string can work wonders with a motor car, but they are poor substitutes for mechanical repairs. Agreement on a formula of compromise to be interpreted by each side in a different sense may end the immediate controversy, but often only by storing up fuel for a later and more violent conflagration. Christ 'is the Prince of Peace, because He, alone among men, never

[1] Küstlin, *Life of Luther*. Quoted by H. E. Fosdick, *On Being a Real Person*, p. 160.

accepted any terms or agreed to any truce in the warfare for truth and righteousness'.[1] Peace making ought to mean dealing with causes, not only with symptoms. It is often thought of as intervening in a quarrel; it ought to mean preventing a quarrel from arising at all.

If we understand 'peace' in the Christian sense—and it is not only in Stockholm and Warsaw that the word has been abused—then the Christian is committed to peacemaking wherever peace is threatened. In international relations, certainly, for the Christian cannot help hating the devilries of war; but we are called to be peacemakers also in the home and all personal relations, in the Church, and as citizens in the State. To cleanse us of self-righteousness, let us remember that most of the divisions and conflicts of mankind have been reproduced and even justified within the borders of the Churches: race divisions, persecution of each other and of those of other faiths, the justification of war for political ends, and the like. The Church has not yet learned to be the Church.

Let us take for brief comment, where each would need a book to itself, two very different but very important fields for Christian peacemaking—the home and international affairs.

One field in which Christians must be peacemakers is that of marriage and the family. No intelligent person can be blind to the grave national situation in this vital and fundamental matter. The steadily rising graph of divorce cases is itself sufficient to cause alarm.[2] Without taking the position that divorce is never justifiable, it must be recognised that every divorce is an admission of failure at a central point of human life and reflects tragic suffering for the couple

[1] Oman, *Grace and Personality*, p. 102.

[2] The latest returns of the Registrar-General show that in 1949 over 34,000 decrees were granted. This is a large reduction on the 52,000 for 1947 but is to be compared with 15,000 decrees in 1945 and 4,500 in 1935. There were 16,000 separation orders in 1949 in addition to the divorces.

concerned and for any children who may be involved. Behind each divorce is a long process of quarrelling and disagreement and mal-adjustment in the home. Much juvenile delinquency and psychological malady in children can be traced to unhappy and insecure home life. No Christian could treat lightly or jokingly such a state of affairs. It should be a chief concern of the Christian citizen —both as Christian and as citizen—to try to help in the achievement of successful marriage and to promote reconciliation where breakdown is threatened.

We ought not to wait until the issue of divorce arises and concentrate on debate as to whether divorce is permissible and if so on what grounds. Our Christian concern should begin much further back. Instruction and guidance in preparation for marriage should be available for all young people. Ministers can help greatly here in dealing with those who come to be married, both by personal advice and through literature.[1] But preparation for marriage should begin in the home, the school, the club, and the church long before the couple comes to put up the banns.

When trouble arises in married life very often sympathetic help would be welcomed by one or both before the situation gets beyond repair. 'It is a public duty to do everything possible to prevent the tragedy of the broken home, and the train of evils which it initiates, by the provision of sympathetic and expert treatment for the prevention and cure of marital disharmony.' That is one of the principles of the Marriage Guidance Council, which is doing splendid work in this field of preparation and reconciliation, both nationally and through its 100 affiliated local councils. The Council should be supported in every possible way by Christians, both by using its expert help when needed, and financially by subscriptions. Much can be done and is being done to heal threatened marriages and to promote the

[1] Many have been greatly helped by being led to read Herbert Gray's *Men, Women and God* (S.C.M. Press).

physical, mental, and spiritual harmony of husband and wife.[1]

But there is much to be done by the ordinary Christian who is not an expert. By word and example we must maintain high ideals of sex relations and family life, and do our utmost to discourage all the influences that cheapen them. The attitude that reveals itself in conversation and jokes and entertainments and literature may depress or raise our national standard of home life. The complaisant acceptance by so much public opinion of low moral standards in sex relations and family life is itself a contributory cause of our serious situation. Every Christian should feel the obligation to act by word and example within his range of influence.

It is very necessary to bear in mind the warnings above against spurious peacemaking when one comes to international relations. So often, for example, it sounds broadminded and Christian to say that both sides in a quarrel are to blame: it may be merely silly. Perhaps both sides are to blame but not necessarily equally, or even to any comparable degree. Moral judgments must often be taken in situations where the right is not all on one side. And if it takes two to make a quarrel it also takes two to make a peace.

The tragedy is that the peacemaker is at times so shut up in a situation, which perhaps he has inherited and for which he may be very little to blame, that he cannot without disloyalty to Christ avoid taking up arms. Yet he cannot delude himself into believing that war itself is anything but hateful and un-Christian. The only alternatives open seem even more hateful and un-Christian. Unilateral disarmament is certainly very unlikely to promote peace in the world as it is. No doubt there is a sense in which armaments may be a cause of war, but in a deeper sense they are only symptoms of a poisonous condition of the body politic.

[1] Apply to the Secretary, 78 Duke Street, London, W.1, where suitable literature can also be obtained.

No one, or at least no nation, fights for the sake of fighting. Nations fight to secure ends which they think cannot be secured in any other way. They may be bad ends like domination or a monopoly of raw materials. It may be a war of sheer brigandage and piracy. But sometimes there are real grievances to be remedied. A nation may seek an outlet for an overcrowded population, markets for unemployed workers, freedom from oppression, racial justice. It may well be wrong in thinking that anything worth having can be secured by war. But clearly the true way of making peace is to deal with the injustices that rankle or to convince the aggrieved party either that it is suffering no injustice at all or one that cannot be remedied. There is abundant evidence of the ways in which a real injustice can be maliciously exploited by ill will. This is the importance of what may be called the side work of the United Nations in promoting economic justice, health, adequate food supplies, and racial and religious equality. Help from more fortunate countries for the development of backward lands is an important contribution to peace making. 'The work of righteousness shall be peace, and the effect of justice shall be security' (Isa. 32.17).

Modern communications make it more possible today than ever to produce a real world fellowship and a fair and efficient world order. But science has not only brought us into one neighbourhood: it has also presented us with the possibilities of self-destruction on an unprecedented scale. The United Nations and its associate organisations are promoting collaboration between the nations more fully than ever. Yet mankind is in two armed camps and still more dreadful world war haunts us all and its possibility is a topic for open discussion everywhere.

Some accept disaster as inevitable. Some are for desperate measures. Some just give it up and relapse into fatalism and fear, often cloaked by a feverish pursuit of pleasure. Christians ought at least to keep their heads. They can never accept the inevitability of war until everything has been done to make peace. And everything has not yet been done. They ought not to be duped by the folly and wickedness of a so-called 'preventive war'. They will not be deceived by glib cries of Peace! Peace! by those who condone aggression. No peace is Christian that does not include freedom and justice or forgets that our goal is a system of world law and order. To that we can travel by more than one road, and Christians should be found on all that really lead there. In the United Nations Association they should be side by side with those who share their ideals, though not all may share their Christian Faith. Christians must care and work and pray at peacemaking in international relations. The situation is one of grave danger: it is also one of great opportunity.[1]

'Blessed are the peacemakers: for they shall be called the children of God.' Men are perhaps more likely to call them traitors, cowards, busybodies, pro-Germans, or fellow travellers. I think Jesus means that God will recognise us as being truly of His family. The Hebrew idiom, 'sons of', means not only descent but sharing the nature and character —as in 'sons of wisdom'. Peacemakers are manifestly sons of God because they bear the Father's likeness. They do as God does. 'Be ye, therefore, imitators of God as beloved children and walk in love.' The Son of God was the Prince of Peace.

---

[1] Some of the last two paragraphs is paraphrased from an excellent U.N.A. pamphlet, *Which Road to Peace?* (9d.), by Alan de Rusett, which is itself a summary of a larger book by the same author, *Strengthening the Framework of Peace*, published by the Royal Institute of International Affairs (21s.). I would also commend two pamphlets *Is it Peace?* and *Christians and World Affairs* (6d. each) published by the British Council of Churches, 39 Doughty Street, London, W.C.1, in which fundamental Christian principles are discussed and a valuable outline given of specific ways in which the Churches corporately and Christians individually are promoting and may continue to promote the cause of peace.

IX

Blessed are they which are persecuted for righteousness' sake: for theirs is the Kingdom of heaven. Blessed
are ye when men shall revile you and persecute you
and shall say all manner of evil against you falsely for
my sake. Rejoice and be exceeding glad, for great is
your reward in heaven: for so persecuted they the
prophets which were before you (Matt. 5.10-12).
Blessed are ye, when men shall hate you, and when
they shall separate you from their company and shall
reproach you, and cast out your name as evil, for the
Son of Man's sake. Rejoice ye in that day and leap
for joy: for behold your reward is great in heaven: for
in the like manner did their fathers unto the prophets
(Luke 6.20-23).[1]

AFTER outlining the kind of character that should be found
in His men and women, Jesus added this most paradoxical
of all the Beatitudes. Matthew Henry says that He repeated
it twice because it sounded incredible!

Our Lord expected His followers to get into trouble and
often warned them to be ready for it (cf. Mark 13.9-13). If
you are this kind of man, He seems to say, do not expect to
be popular or to find life easy. You will certainly be hated,
sneered at, and persecuted, but even in that you can be
victorious and find cause for rejoicing. It has been suggested
by some scholars that these warnings reflect a later period
of church life, but the note is sounded so frequently in the
Gospels and is so in harmony with Jesus' own experience
that there is no reason to think that it is not authentic. To
Jesus, loyalty to God and righteousness involved sacrifice
and suffering. In much of the Old Testament prosperity is

[1] Note that Luke lists four kinds of persecution: hatred, isolation or
excommunication, reproach and slander. Manson (*Sayings of Jesus*,
p. 48) says that 'cast out your name as evil' means 'issue an evil report
about you'.

regarded as a mark of the Divine favour: Jesus said 'Woe unto you when all men shall speak well of you'. 'Whereas at the Bible's beginning the practice of religion is in large measure a means of escaping trouble, at the Bible's end the practice of religion is a sure means of getting into trouble.'[1]

And of course Christians *have* got into trouble for their faith. The noble army of martyrs has marched through all the centuries and numbers in its ranks men and women of every nation and race. If you are persecuted you are in good company: that was the fate of the prophets before you. Note that persecution 'for righteousness sake' is equated with persecution 'for my sake'. Here is implied a tremendous claim by Jesus for Himself; one more evidence that the Sermon on the Mount is not so 'simple' and free from awkward theological complications as some folk would have us believe.

St. Paul knew the inner meaning of persecution from both sides. Before Christ met him on the Damascus road he persecuted the Church of God (I Cor. 15.9; Acts 22.7ff.; Phil. 3.6) but he came to feel the lash on his own body and knew the restraint of bonds for Christ's sake. And he had learned from Jesus how to take it (Rom. 12.14; I Cor. 4.12; II Cor. 4.9). 'Insomuch as ye are partakers of Christ's sufferings, rejoice', wrote St. Peter.[2] There is a good deal in his First Epistle about 'the fiery trial' and how it is to be faced. It is nothing to be surprised at: it is only what Christians must expect. And 'if ye are reproached for the name of Christ blessed are ye': surely a reminiscence of the Beatitude, using the same Greek word for 'blessed'.[3]

Only limitations of space prevent one from recording such testimonies from all the succeeding centuries and from

[1] Fosdick, *A Guide to Understanding the Bible*, p. 199.

[2] I think we are justified, in spite of denials, in accepting the Petrine origin of the Epistle, while allowing that its form and style probably owes much to his 'secretary', Silvanus.

[3] I Pet. 4.14. R.V. Note vv. 12-16. See comments in *The First Epistle of Peter*, by C. E. B. Cranfield (S.C.M. Press).

many lands. Here, for example, is Francis of Assisi discoursing to Friar Leo about the 'perfect joy' that is to be found in enduring suffering for Christ's sake: 'And now, Friar Leo, hear the conclusion. Above all the grace and the gifts of the Holy Spirit that Christ giveth to His beloved is that of overcoming self, and for love of Him willingly to bear pain and buffeting, and revilings and discomfort.'[1]

Think again of John Bunyan, a very different kind of man in a very different setting. This Beatitude is printed on the title-page of his autobiographical book: *A Relation of the Imprisonment of Mr. John Bunyan, Minister of the Gospel.*[2] It was in its spirit that he faced his long sufferings.

Samuel Rutherfurd declared: 'I never knew by my nine years preaching so much of Christ's love as He taught me in Aberdeen by six months imprisonment.' 'Christ's Cross', he said, 'is such a burden as sails are to a ship or wings to a bird.'

John and Charles Wesley, and their helpers, knew persecution even to the danger of life and limb, and the meaning of this Beatitude. 'Ye servants of God, your Master proclaim' was written 'to be sung in a tumult'—not a quiet pew.

> The waves of the sea have lift up their voice
> Sore troubled that we in Jesus rejoice;
> The floods they are soaring, but Jesus is here;
> While we are adoring, He always is near.

'Soldiers of Christ arise' was also written in time of persecution and is instinct with battle.

Henry Martyn in India tells of how his teaching of the divinity of Christ 'exposes me to the contempt of the learned Mohammedans. . . . Their sneers are more difficult to bear than the brickbats which the boys sometimes throw at me; however, both are an honour of which I am not

[1] *The Little Flowers of St. Francis*, Everyman Edition, p. 16.

[2] First published in 1765, nearly a hundred years after his death in 1688. See *The Works of John Bunyan.* Edited by George Offor. Vol. I. pp. 50ff.

worthy.' Later in Persia he had the same experience. 'What have I done, thought I, to merit all this scorn? Nothing, I trust, but bear testimony to Jesus. I thought over these things in prayer, and found that peace which Christ has promised to His disciples.'

The list of quotations might go on into the last ten years. The victims of the Gestapo found the promise of Jesus true in conditions we cannot bear even to read about. But let the selection of illustrations—a selection from hundreds that might be given—close with a testimony from Sadhu Sundar Singh in India. 'His presence gives me a Peace which passeth all understanding, no matter in what circumstances I am placed. Amidst persecution I have found peace, joy and happiness. Nothing can take away the joy I have found in my Saviour. In home He was there. In Him the prison was transformed into heaven and the cross into a source of blessing.'

In many commentaries on the New Testament persecution is spoken of as one of the 'old unhappy far-off things'. To our fathers and grandfathers martyrdom and persecution were stories to be read in a history book or in missionary tales from far away lands. In our own time religious persecution has again become widespread. In country after country the Church of Christ has been facing its test. Many of us have friends in different parts of the world who have suffered persecution for the Faith, perhaps are still suffering. Usually this is at the hands of those who profess some other religion, or of a godless government, but unhappily some of it is due to sections of the Christian Church. Few Christian traditions have clean hands in this matter. Most of us have learned better, but it is shameful to have to record that there are still countries where the dominant Christian Church persecutes others.[1]

In this country, happily, we have not to face imprisonment or physical torture because of our Christian discipleship. We have not 'resisted unto blood' as so many of our contem-

[1] See, e.g., Cecil Northcott, *Religious Liberty*. S.C.M. Press.

poraries have had to do (Heb. 12.4; the whole chapter is relevant). There is little active opposition to the churches. For the most part we are treated with a respectful indifference, or an amused surprise if any of us show any strenuous concern for Christian service. But if hostility hammers, indifference is apt to rust: and rust may well be a more dangerous enemy to metal than blows.

In *English Life and Leisure*, Mr. Seebohm Rowntree and Mr. G. R. Lavers have recently published some facts and judgments about religion, mainly based upon enquiries in York and High Wycombe in 1947. They conclude 'that people today still believe that Christianity is a relevant and vital force although they no longer accept the idea that the Church is the chosen instrument for the expression of that force'. While they therefore find the situation 'somewhat brighter than is popularly believed', they hold it 'certain that people will never again seek from the Churches, in their present form, the inspiration that they should obtain from them'.[1] This suggests a wide diffusion of Christian ideas and values which might account for the absence of positive opposition or persecution. It is certainly true, though it is all too little recognised among us, that much of the best in our Western life comes from Christian sources and that many of our institutions are impregnated with Christian ideals, even when nominally 'secular'. Any first hand knowledge of life in 'non-Christian lands' makes this evident. A recent book by Mr. Kitson Clark, *The English Inheritance* (S.C.M. Press), provides an interesting and valuable study of this.

Another reason for the absence of much active opposition in this country is perhaps that consciously or unconsciously Christians generally have accepted the current standards of value and so narrowed the difference between Christians

[1] Somewhat surprisingly, they also find 'so widespread a dislike of the ministers of religion of the Anglican and Free Churches that it can only be described as anti-clericalism'. This, if generally true, is a new development.

and the ordinary secular man. Are we left alone because we are no longer troublesome? I stayed once with a missionary friend in an Indian city which contains one of the most famous of all Hindu temples. There had been a little Christian Church there for a hundred years, but the Temple and its festivals seemed as secure as ever. The head, and I think hereditary owner, of the temple called at my friend's house. I told him I was touring India on behalf of the Student Christian Movement. He asked many questions, and insisted, with great kindness, that I should accept the loan of his carriage and driver on the following day in order that I might visit places of interest in the neighbourhood. When he had gone I turned to my friend, in surprise: 'Tell me', I said, 'why he is so friendly. He knows that you and I are here to put him out of business.' 'Ah', said my friend sadly, 'He knows we are not really dangerous. . . .' If we were more effective in Christian living and advocacy in Britain, if we became dangerous to vested interests, might persecution become a reality again?

It is, of course, obviously unsafe to assume that if we are unpopular it is because of our Christianity. The Beatitude applies only to people accused falsely, and to persecution for Christ's sake. It does not apply to the 'unco' guid', to the provocation aroused by offensive manners and self-assertion, by needless angularity and harsh priggish judgment. There are Christians who go about asking for trouble and get disliked not because of their Christianity but for their lack of it. We should be cautious in counting ourselves among the martyrs. There are false prophets and false martyrs in every generation.

Christian witness-bearing is a difficult task, even with complete sincerity and humility. 'The real difficulty of preaching the Gospel of God's mercy to the prodigal son, represented by our modern culture, lies in the temptation to play the part of the elder brother. No Christian Church has a right to preach to an age which we call secular without a contrite recognition of the shortcomings of historic

Christianity, which are one cause of the disavowal by the modern age of its Christian faith'.[1]

Yet ought we not to be coming into conflict with public opinion and with accepted ways of thought and life? Christian moral standards are generally disregarded today. The motives normally appealed to are not those that Christ would endorse. Dean Inge often asserted that Christians have always been and must always be in a minority. It is complained, he wrote, that our churches are empty, but they would be emptier still if the Gospel was preached in them. That is certainly a gloomy suggestion. But is it true?

Certainly a thoroughgoing Christianity would demand great changes in our modern ways of life. Ought we not to be a little unhappy if all men speak well of us, and ask ourselves the reason? Christians even in Britain are—and always have been—a minority in a pagan world. And now the world no longer even pretends to be Christian. Is not a living Christian a rebuke to wrong? If his witness does not win the enemy will it not provoke him to attack? Granted that we ought not to go seeking persecution and unpopularity, ought they not sometimes to seek us? If we have *never* suffered for our Faith, is there not something wrong with our witness? Universal popularity is not often the sign of a determined Christian character. Lukewarmness never shocks. 'A true Christian', wrote Alexander MacLaren on this Beatitude, 'ought to be a standing rebuke to the world, an incarnate conscience. There are but two ways of ending that antagonism: either by bringing the world up to Christian character, or letting Christian character down to the world.' Goodness does not always win its way. We would all rather believe that there is a universal innate love of goodness, and that the character of the Beatitudes would surely disarm opposition. But Jesus knew and experienced that there is deliberate opposition to good.

The Wisdom of Solomon long ago set out this antagonism

[1] J. H. Oldham in *The Churches Survey Their Task*, p. 36.

between the 'ungodly man' and 'the righteous man' (1.16-2.20). Making spoil of life for their selfish ends and exploiting the poor and weak for their pleasure, the ungodly come up against the righteous man.

> He is of disservice to us,
> And is contrary to our works,
> And upbraideth us with sins against the law

> He became to us a reproof of our thoughts.
> He is grievous unto us even to behold,
> Because his life is unlike other men's,
> And his paths are of strange fashion.

And so they plot to do him evil.

The average man is apt to be intolerant of a Christian who takes his religion 'too' seriously. Insistence on high standards of Christian morality in business or social life often lead to unpopularity, or worse. Read again Bunyan's witty and searching account of the trial of Faithful in Vanity Fair. 'Then said Mr. No-good, "Away with such a fellow from the earth". "Ay", said Mr. Malice, "for I hate the very look of him." Then said Mr. Love-Lust, "I could never endure him". "Nor I", said Mr. Live-loose, "for he would always be condemning my way." ' And the rest of the jury were of the same mind. They are still with us. Perhaps they are to be found in our office or works or club.

Many people who are sincere Christians do face a kind of persecution. There are other methods than the rack or the thumbscrew: the sneer of the club or the office or the home or the barracks is almost harder to meet. We do not throw Christians to the lions but we sometimes send them to Coventry. It is hard to be reckoned a spoil sport and a prig because one doesn't welcome the indecent story or refuses to accept recognised sharp practices or stands out of the office sweepstake.

'Universal reproach', wrote John Milton, 'is far worse to bear than violence.' 'Compared with the contempt of mankind', declared Adam Smith. 'all other external evils are easily supported.' It takes real courage for young people to take a Christian stand today in many homes and work-shops and offices. 'God hath called you to Christ's side', wrote Samuel Rutherfurd to a friend, 'and the wind is now in Christ's face in this land; and seeing ye are with Him ye cannot expect the lee side or the sunny side of the brae.'

'Rejoice and be exceeding glad', said Jesus. Is not that asking too much? Incredible as it seems the martyrs have in fact rejoiced. Men who have had to suffer for their witness have often told us that faith became more real to them, and that they knew in their suffering the presence of Christ. From Paul and Silas, soundly beaten and put in stocks in the inner prison, there came songs at midnight (Acts 16.22-25). A strange occasion, place, and time for singing, one would think. But their song has been taken up down the ages, as the illustrations earlier in the chapter have shown. There is apparently an exhilaration that comes to those who have given the world away and risked their all for Christ. 'Why persecutest thou *me*?', said the Risen Lord to the man who was harrying His humble disciples. Where two or three are persecuted for His sake, there is He in the midst of them.

The Beatitude gives the persecuted three grounds for rejoicing. Persecution for Christ's sake is evidence that they are freemen of the Kingdom of God. They are in good company with the prophets and martyrs of the Church. There shall be for them a great reward in heaven.

'Theirs is the Kingdom of Heaven', as is said also of the poor in spirit. As was pointed out in commenting on that Beatitude (p. 33), 'heaven' in this phrase is a Jewish and Matthaean way of saying 'God', and does not mean the future life. To be citizens in the Kingdom of God is to be at home in God's family, in the enjoyment of His love, and in fellowship with all His other sons and daughters.

The persecuted are in the best of company, with the goodly fellowship of the prophets and the noble army of martyrs. Even the humble private in the ranks shows himself to have something of their spirit. And Jesus Himself met persecution. Let one reminder suffice. He healed a man in the synagogue on the Sabbath day, 'and the Pharisees went forth and straightway took counsel with the Herodians to destroy Him' (Mark 3.6). He was the Captain of Faith, the leader of all the glorious company of whom the eleventh chapter of the Epistle to the Hebrews tells.

And great will be their reward in heaven. Bunyan knows that the cruel death of Faithful at the stake in Vanity Fair is not the end for him. 'Now I saw that there stood behind the multitude a chariot and a couple of horses waiting for Faithful, who (so soon as his adversaries had despatched him) was taken up into it, and straightway was carried up through the clouds with sound of trumpet, the nearest way to the celestial gate.' The Church triumphant welcomes the martyr to the 'solemn troops and sweet societies' of the heavenly city.

Perhaps if we took Christianity more seriously we should find life a much more cheerful affair than we do. It is so difficult to go on being half-Christian and half-pagan. 'The greatest mistake the Church has ever made—and it has pervaded its history—is that of concealing from the young and from men in general that Christianity is not an easy thing. . . . The Christian life is a way of adventure, a difficult way, a way that requires courage.' The words are those of Bishop Gore. If we find them exaggerated and if Christianity seems to us tame, conventional, and respectable it might be well to ponder more than we do the Beatitudes of the Lord Jesus.

EPILOGUE

Portrait of a Christian

HE stands before God in humble gratitude, making no claims, knowing he owes everything to the divine bounty.

He is moved with compassion for the grief and suffering of his fellow men.

His life is devoted to the service of God's Kingdom, not to seeking his own ends. He can be determined and aggressive and angry when the weak are oppressed, but he is never self-assertive or angry at slights to himself.

He longs with intensity for the triumph of goodness in his own life and in the life of the world, with a longing as strong and as much a part of his spiritual life as hunger and thirst are in the life of his body.

But he is not censorious or critical of those who fail, knowing his own weakness. He will not break the bruised reed, but seeks to mend it. He is moved to mercy.

He is single minded in devotion to God and the things of God.

A lover of peace, he takes the spirit of reconciliation with him wherever he goes.

Some respond to him but some resent his presence, as a rebuke to their way of life or a threat to their selfish interests. If persecution comes he finds cause for gladness even in that, because he remembers that Jesus trod that way and that he can fill up something of what is lacking in His sufferings. And he knows he marches with a great and noble company.

Such a man is truly blessed. He has learned the secret of true living. He is a citizen of God's Kingdom, counted by Him as a true son. He lives in the conscious presence of God. Though poor he possesses all things and savours all the beauty and worth of his Father's world. A strength not his own sustains him. The divine love and forgiveness are his.

He grows in goodness and is heartened by the knowledge that in God's own time the cause of good will triumph. He belongs to the company of the prophets and martyrs and for him the trumpets of welcome shall sound at the gates of heaven.

We have never seen this man, but some we have known have reminded us of him.

Only once has such as he walked among us, full of grace and truth: Jesus Himself, the originator and perfect example of our Faith, the Christian Man.

APPENDIX

Other New Testament Beatitudes

THE Beatitude form is to be found in several other sayings of Jesus. Possibly it was a characteristic of His way of teaching.

Blessed is he, whosoever shall find none occasion of stumbling in me (Matt. 11.6; cf. Luke 7.23).

Blessed are your eyes for they see (Matt. 13.16; cf. Luke 10.23).

Blessed art thou, Simon Bar Jona (Matt. 16.17).

Come ye blessed of my Father (Matt. 25.34). (A different Greek word for 'blessed' is used here).

Blessed are they that hear the word of God and keep it (Luke 11.28).

Blessed are those servants whom the Lord when He cometh shall find watching (Luke 12.37).

When thou makest a feast, call the poor, the maimed, the lame, the blind: and thou shalt be blessed (Luke 14.13).

If ye know these things, happy are ye if ye do them (John 13.17). (The word translated 'happy' is the word translated 'blessed' in the Beatitudes.)

Blessed are they that have not seen and yet have believed (John 20.29).

It is more blessed to give than to receive (Acts 20.35). Cf. also Blessed are the dead which die in the Lord (Rev. 14.3).

Outside the New Testament are one or two other Beatitudes attributed to Jesus.

Codex Bezae at Luke 6.4. has: 'On the same day seeing one working on the Sabbath, he said unto him: "If thou knowest what thou doest, thou art blessed; but if thou knowest not, thou art under a curse, and a transgressor of the law." '

In the apocryphal *Acts of Paul* which Tertullian says was forged by a presbyter who was convicted of the imposture, about A.D. 160, Paul is represented as uttering a whole series of Beatitudes, including two from the Gospel but with several clearly coloured by the author's ascetic tendencies.

QUESTIONS FOR DISCUSSION ON THE BEATITUDES

I

1. 'If the churches would drop their complicated theological dogmas and preach the simple and sublime religion of the Sermon on the Mount and the Beatitudes, they would make a powerful appeal to the modern man.' Discuss.

2. The author says: 'If the Christian God is denied Christian moral standards will not long survive.' Do you agree?

3. It is argued that Christianity defeats its own ends by making an impossibly high moral demand. An ethical code that was generally attainable would be more practically helpful. What have you to say to this?

II

1. What do you gather from the Gospels as to the attitude of Jesus to money?

2. Do you agree with the author's interpretation of the 'poor in spirit'? Does pride deserve its place at the head of the seven deadly sins?

III

1. Do sorrow and suffering purify the soul?

2. 'It is a blessing upon those who mourn for the needs of others, whose hearts are full of sympathy for their fellows.' Do you agree? Does religion make people sympathetic?

IV

1. 'To bear wrong uncomplainingly may not be a Christian virtue at all; it may be cowardice or moral indifference.' Ought a Christian always to be gentle and patient? When, if ever, is it right to be angry?

2. What do you think Jesus meant by inheriting the earth?

V

1. Is it true that before God can feed the soul there must be hunger?

2. 'You cannot put Christian righteousness into a Decalogue.' Why not?

VI

1. 'There is something wrong with our following of Jesus if it makes us hard and denunciatory.' Do you think that Christian campaigns for, say, Sunday observance or temperance are sometimes open to this criticism?

2. Do you think men generally are growing more or less pitiful?

VII

1. Is it true that we can 'see God in the beauty of nature and of human nature'? Some theologians dispute it.

2. 'How greatly Jesus valued sincerity. It comes out again and again in the Gospels.' Can you find illustrations of this?

VIII

1. 'All human quarrels are at bottom symptoms of a broken peace with God.' Do you think this is true? Or is it merely a fine-sounding, pious remark?

2. Can you tabulate some tests of Christian peacemaking to distinguish it from spurious imitations?

3. What could the Church do to promote higher ideals of marriage in the nation?

INDEX

A. Biblical References

B. NAMES AND SUBJECTS